FLOWER GARDENS

Dear Friend,

IN THE LATE 1950s, THE SCOTTS COMPANY RAN AN ADVERTISEMENT featuring a happy homeowner with a Scotts® lawn-fertilizer spreader. The headline announced that this was a "Man With a Plan!" We wanted to let people know that the most foolproof way to have a beautiful lawn was to follow a plan that provided feedings, weedings, waterings, and other basics throughout the growing season. My wife, Nancy, and I have been following that great advice on our own lawn for the 23 years I've been here at Scotts. All of those years, though, we've wished someone would come along and tell us how we could easily fill the rest of our yard with flowers, shrubs, groundcovers, trees, and other beautiful plants. Now we can—and you can, too—with the Scotts *See & Do Solutions*™ series of lawn and garden books.

These books fit well with the philosophy Scotts has always embraced: making lawn and garden care a breeze. Each 128-page book presents 50 easy-to-follow garden plans designed to help you solve the challenges in your own yard. To help meet your needs, every plan is suited to sunny or shady conditions, climate, location in the yard, or a specific landscaping situation. Each plan gives you an illustrated garden map and a "recipe" you can follow to get the effect you see in the full-color photograph—complete with an "ingredient" list that tells you exactly how many of each plant you'll need. Scotts has done all of the planning, so you don't have to. Having a beautiful yard couldn't be any easier!

With this book in hand, you, too, are now a person with a plan. Happy gardening!

Tadd C Seitz

Tadd C. Seitz
Chairman, The Scotts Company

P.S. We'd love to hear from you. Call us at 1-800-543-TURF with your questions.

Contents

On the cover: See pages 6 and 7.

How to Use This Book

THIS BOOK WAS DESIGNED WITH BUSY GARDENERS IN MIND. WE KNOW THAT YOU WANT a beautiful yard but don't necessarily have the time to dissect a difficult-to-read volume. That's why we made it simple. These pages explain the easy-to-use features of this book.

What sets this book apart are the 50 beautiful garden plans featured on pages 6-95. A sample of one of those pages is shown on the opposite page.

Many of the book's remaining sections are designed to equip you with the additional know-how you might need to install the plans in your own yard. For example, in the back of the book is a Flower Basics section that gives you the how-to knowledge you need to plant and maintain the flowers described in the plans.

On pages 116-118, you'll find answers to the most commonly asked questions about flower gardening. And on pages 119-123, you'll find the Plant Alternatives section—a listing of replacement plants that are hardy in regions other than those listed on the plan pages. This makes it possible for you to use nearly all of the plans, no matter where you live. If you're stumped by one of the common names shown on the plans, use the index to find the corresponding botanical name.

As an additional feature, on each plan page we've left some space to let you write notes about your garden. And in the very back of the book is a handy pocket to hold notes, seed packets, or garden-plant tags.

As a special gift from Scotts® to get your gardening off to the right start, we've included certificates on pages 127 and 128 for savings on a selection of Scotts high-quality lawn and gardening products at your local Scotts retailer.

CLIMATE REGIONS

A	Cold-Winter Climates (-40°F to 0°F)
B	Mild-Winter Climates (0°F to 20°F)
C	Warm-Winter Climates (20°F to 40°F)

The three regions shown on this **climate-region map** refer to cold-, mild-, and warm-winter climates. The temperatures shown in the key are minimum annual temperatures. With your region in mind, you'll quickly be able to access the plans in this book that—as shown— fit your area. Or, use your region designation and the listings on pages 119-123 to find alternatives to the plants shown.

The **question-and-answer** format identifies real problems just like the kind you may well have in your yard. The question asks how to solve it, and the answer tells you how. It also presents some alternative suggestions.

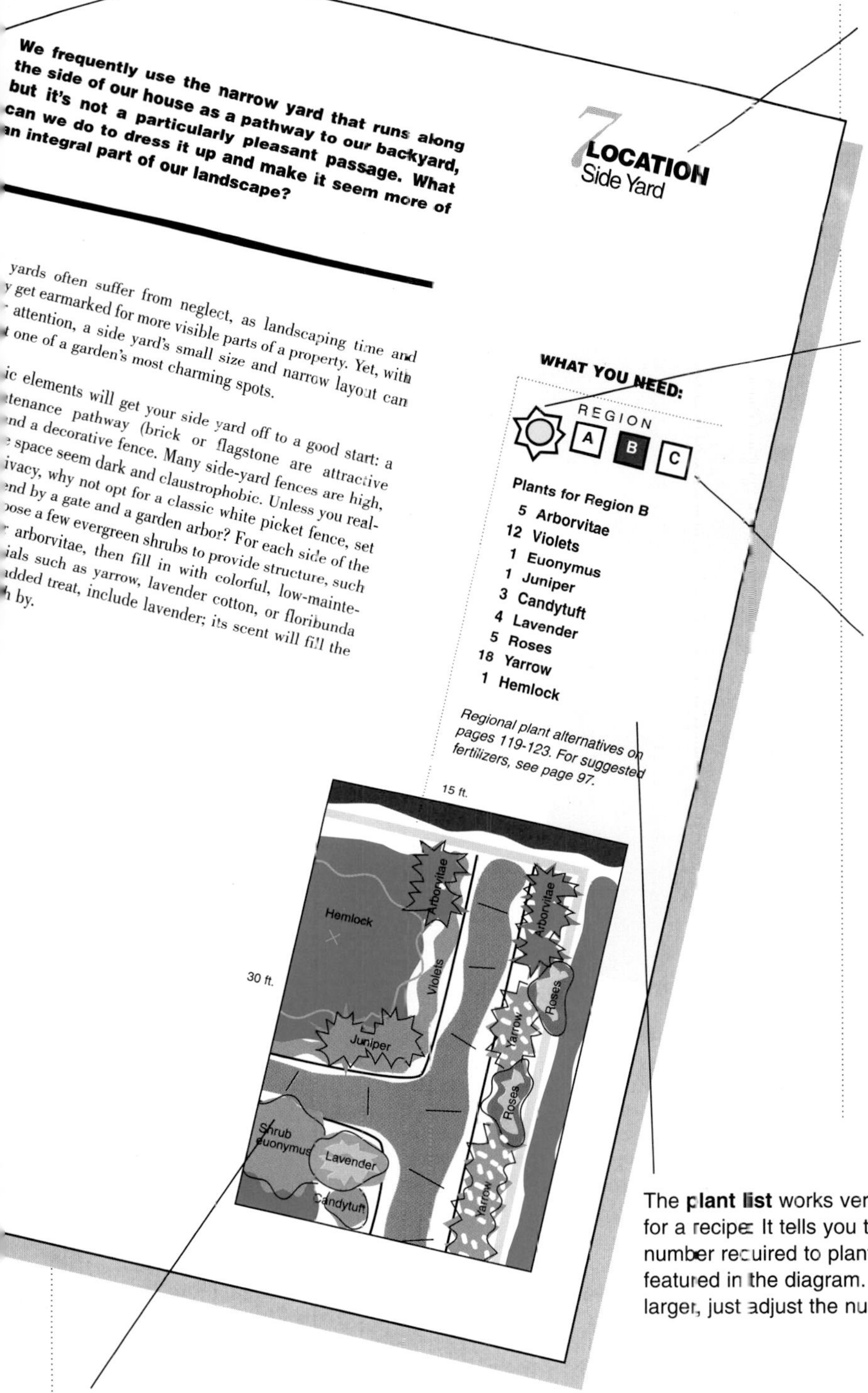

The **headlines** in the upper corner of each plan page help you quickly tell if a plan fits your needs.

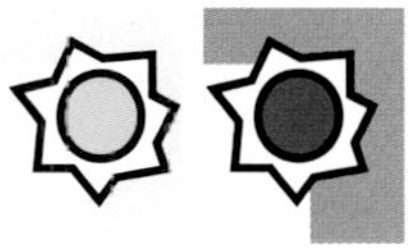

We frequently use the narrow yard that runs along the side of our house as a pathway to our backyard, but it's not a particularly pleasant passage. What can we do to dress it up and make it seem more of an integral part of our landscape?

7 **LOCATION**
Side Yard

A yellow **sun icon** on the plan page indicates the plan is suited for sun conditions. The color bar also will be yellow if the plan is designed for a sun garden. If the sun icon is shaded and the color bar is blue, the plan is suited to a shade garden.

yards often suffer from neglect, as landscaping time and y get earmarked for more visible parts of a property. Yet, with attention, a side yard's small size and narrow layout can one of a garden's most charming spots.

ic elements will get your side yard off to a good start: a tenance pathway (brick or flagstone are attractive e space seem dark and claustrophobic. Many side-yard fences are high, ivacy, why not opt for a classic white picket fence, set nd by a gate and a garden arbor? For each side of the ose a few evergreen shrubs to provide structure, such r arborvitae, then fill in with colorful, low-mainte-ials such as yarrow, lavender cotton, or floribunda added treat, include lavender; its scent will fill the h by.

WHAT YOU NEED:

REGION
A B C

Plants for Region B
5 Arborvitae
12 Violets
1 Euonymus
1 Juniper
3 Candytuft
4 Lavender
5 Roses
18 Yarrow
1 Hemlock

Regional plant alternatives on pages 119-123. For suggested fertilizers, see page 97.

These **lettered boxes** correspond to our three climate regions. The "A" box is for cold-winter climates; the "B" box is for mild-winter climates; and the "C" box is for warm-winter climates. On each plan, one or more of these boxes will be green, telling you that the plan is suited to those particular regions. Don't forget to check the Plant Alternatives section on pages 119-123. With the help of these lists, nearly all of the plans are adaptable to any region of the country.

15 ft.

Hemlock

Arborvitae

Arborvitae

Violets

Roses

30 ft.

Juniper

Yarrow

Roses

Shrub Euonymus

Lavender

Yarrow

Candytuft

The **plant list** works very much like the ingredient list for a recipe. It tells you the plants you'll need and the number required to plant a garden the size of the one featured in the diagram. If your space is smaller or larger, just adjust the number of plants accordingly.

The **garden-plan illustration** is a to-scale, overhead view of the garden featured in the photograph. It clearly shows you how to lay out your garden to get the kinds of effects you see in the photograph. Remember, the gardens in the photographs have been cultivated over a number of years. Follow our plans and be patient. You'll get there, too.

Q: Most of my yard is well landscaped, but the area where the lawn meets the sidewalk needs help. I'd particularly like to have more flowers to brighten our long springtime. Would that be a good spot?

A: The sunny slope where your lawn and sidewalk meet couldn't be a better location for a bright edging of annual flowers. With well-timed planting and a warmer climate, flowers will bloom there from winter through spring and into early summer.

The key for many early-bloomers in warm parts of the country is fall planting. When planted as seed or set out in September or early October, plants have a chance to establish healthy roots during winter rains, then are ready to burst into bloom at the first hint of warmth. Favorites for such treatment include calendula and larkspur, both of which can be planted as seed. Striking color and blooms also can be had from Iceland poppy or snapdragon (dwarf or tall varieties), which should be set out as nursery starts. When planning your plantings, think in terms of bold, broad swaths of color; too many different plants in a small area will create a chaotic, spotty look.

WHAT YOU NEED:

REGION
A B C

Plants for Regions A, B, & C

- 30 **Snapdragons**
- 9 **Larkspur**
- 18 **Calendula**
- 6 **Iceland poppies**
- 3 **Columbine**

Regional plant alternatives on pages 119-123. For suggested fertilizers, see page 97.

19 ft.

30 ft.

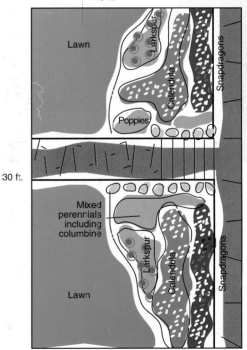

Q: The wide brick walkway that leads to our front door is so drab it makes our whole house look dreary. I'd love to incorporate more color. Is there an easy way to add more glamour to this plain-looking spot?

A: Your grass-flanked front walk is tailor-made for floral edgings, brimming with annuals and fragrant with roses. Prepare the beds by removing a strip of grass 2 to 3 feet in width from along both sides of the walkway. Turn the soil to a depth of 1 foot or more, incorporating plenty of dampened peat moss and decomposed organic matter, such as leaves or manure. To keep the grass from encroaching, border outer edges of the beds with pressure-treated lumber held in place with wooden stakes.

In the early spring, space an equal number of bare-root floribunda roses at intervals along each side of the walkway. 'Iceberg' is one good choice, beloved for its pure white blooms. (See pages 106-109 for tips on planting and caring for roses.) Fill beds in between with a mix of easy-care annuals—brilliant purple lobelia, airy sweet alyssum, and bright pink ivy geranium; they'll provide blooms throughout the summer months. To lend extra glamour at night, line the walk with low-voltage lights.

WHAT YOU NEED:

REGION

A B C

Plants for Regions A, B, & C

- 8 **Lobelia**
- 6 **Sweet alyssum**
- 12 **Ivy geraniums**
- 12 **Roses**

Regional plant alternatives on pages 119-123. For suggested fertilizers, see page 97.

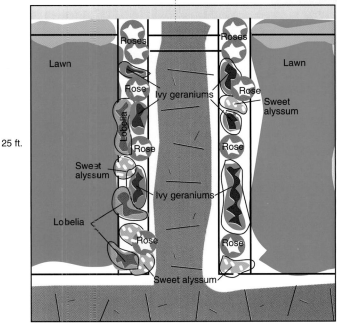

25 ft.

25 ft.

WHAT YOU NEED:

REGION

A   B   C

Plants for Regions A, B, & C

- 3 Roses
- 3 Climbing roses
- 6 Pinks
- 3 Daylilies
- 7 Lilies
- 3 Lavender
- 5 Campanula
- 6 *Verbena bonariensis*
- 8 Petunias

Regional plant alternatives on pages 119-123. For suggested fertzilizers, see page 97.

Q: We would like the entrance to our home to be a real show-stopper, but the landscaping is pretty mundane. I have always loved the cottage gardens of England; can we create that look on a small scale here?

A: The romantic look of many dooryard gardens in the British Isles has more to do with a happy profusion of plants than with any particular nuance of soil or climate. Such a plan is well suited to a traditional-style home, particularly if you take advantage of classic cottage plants, such as climbing roses. (See pages 106-109 for tips on growing roses.)

Begin by setting aside a rectangular, half-moon-shape, or triangular plot on each side of your entry. Choose a variety of perennials suited to your climate and soil. Include an assortment of heights and shapes, from the tall spikes of foxglove to low mounds of lavender. For a particularly carefree look, include some plants that tower above the others, such as *Verbena bonariensis*. Tuck climbing roses strategically alongside the doorway; by the second year of growth, they'll frame your entry with a glorious display of spicy blooms.

30 ft.

30 ft.

Roses

Pinks

Rose

Daylilies

Mix of lavender, campanula, lilies, and pinks

Verbena

Petunias

Climbing roses

Q: Our house has a certain amount of vintage charm, but our front yard looks like a transplant from a 1960s suburb—it's nothing but sidewalk and lawn. How can we create an approach more suited to the style of our house?

A: Nothing sets a mood of romance faster than an old-fashioned arch over a garden's entrance. Lightweight garden arches often can be found at garden-supply stores. A sturdier structure could be built by a carpenter to fit your particular size requirements.

Once your arbor is securely anchored in place, plant repeat-blooming climbing roses on each side of it slightly behind the structure; train the canes up over the top of the arch as they grow. If desired, plant creeping figs to cover the base of the arbor. To further dress the entry to your yard in vintage style, plant a privet hedge along the sidewalk. Privet hedges are fast-growing, don't mind poor soil, and take readily to shearing; they've been used in this country as a stand-in for fences since the 1700s.

WHAT YOU NEED:

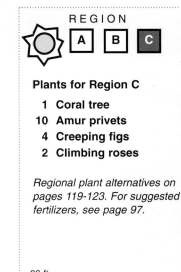

REGION
A B **C**

Plants for Region C

- 1 Coral tree
- 10 Amur privets
- 4 Creeping figs
- 2 Climbing roses

Regional plant alternatives on pages 119-123. For suggested fertilizers, see page 97.

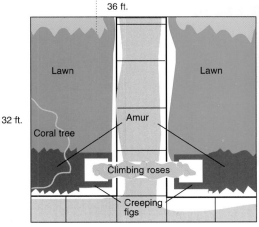

36 ft.

Lawn

Lawn

32 ft.

Coral tree

Amur

Climbing roses

Creeping figs

Q: I've planted lots of spring bulbs and perennials in our yard, but the bed that runs along our front porch is planted with juniper shrubs and stays flowerless throughout the year. I'd like to make a change. Do you have any advice?

A: There's no reason why the shrubs along the foundation of your house shouldn't do double duty, both hiding the underpinnings of your porch and adding floral beauty and fragrance to your yard.

First, take advantage of your porch uprights and use one as a trellis for an evergreen clematis, which will provide heavenly white (or pale pink) flowers during the spring. These fast-growing plants like the sun, but enjoy fast-draining soil and continual moisture. Keep roots cool by heavy mulching, or shade with other shrubbery. For more spring flowers and intoxicating fragrance, plant a row of Mexican oranges along the front of the porch; their clusters of small white flowers look and smell much like orange blossoms. Keep plants well pruned to maintain desired height and form. Lastly, establish a white-on-white edging by planting a bank of evergreen candytuft at the base of the shrubs. To encourage new growth, shear lightly after flowering.

WHAT YOU NEED:

REGION

A   B   C

Plants for Regions B & C

1	Spirea
50	Squill
30	Tulips
12	Candytufts
5	Mexican oranges
2	Evergreen clematis

Regional plant alternatives on pages 119-123. For suggested fertilizers, see page 97.

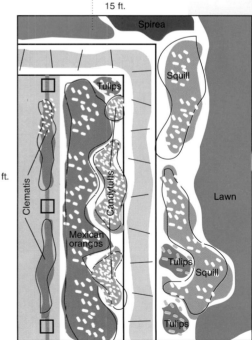

Q: We have a nice lawn and some beautiful trees in our yard, but something's missing. Our house looks too stark and doesn't blend well with the rest of the landscape. How can we gracefully unify the two?

A: Many people rely on evergreen landscaping shrubs, such as cypresses, for foundation plantings. But why not tie your house to the surrounding yard and soften the edges of the structure with a lush bank of flowering perennials? In your mild climate, many will retain their foliage year-round; others will provide a seasonal show of color.

Although strict regimentation isn't necessary or desirable, plan your border to include low-growing plants, such as lamb's ears or coreopsis, along the front of the flower bed, reserving tall plants, such as climbing roses and fennel, for the back. Tuck airy plants, medium-growers, or flowers that float above their foliage in between. Lilies lend a particularly pleasing old-fashioned touch; choose varieties with different bloom periods for continual color. Provide moisture year-round, and protect bulbs in wire baskets if gophers are troublesome in your neighborhood. Cut lilies back to ground level only after foliage has yellowed.

WHAT YOU NEED:

REGION
A B C

Plants for Regions B & C

- 4 Lilies
- 6 Baby's breath
- 3 Coreopsis
- 2 Fennel
- 6 Lamb's ears
- 3 Roses
- 3 Matilija poppies
- 3 Irises
- 5 Allium
- 1 Lavender
- 1 Japanese maple

Regional plant alternatives on pages 119-123. For suggested fertilizers, see page 97.

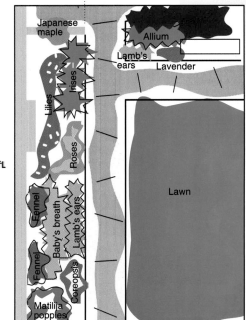

Q: We frequently use the narrow yard that runs along the side of our house as a pathway to our back yard, but it's not a particularly pleasant passage. What can we do to dress it up and make it seem more of an integral part of our landscape?

A: Side yards often suffer from neglect, as landscaping time and money get earmarked for more visible parts of a property. Yet, with proper attention, a side yard's small size and narrow layout can make it one of a garden's most charming spots.

Two basic elements will get your side yard off to a good start: a low-maintenance pathway (brick or flagstone are attractive choices) and a decorative fence. Many side-yard fences are high, making the space seem dark and claustrophobic. Unless you really crave privacy, why not opt for a classic white picket fence, set off at each end by a gate and a garden arbor? For each side of the walkway, choose a few evergreen shrubs to provide structure, such as juniper or arborvitae, then fill in with colorful, low-maintenance perennials, such as yarrow, lavender cotton, or floribunda roses. For an added treat, include lavender; its scent will fill the air as you brush by.

WHAT YOU NEED:

REGION

A **B** C

Plants for Region B

5	Arborvitae
12	Violets
1	Euonymus
1	Juniper
3	Candytuft
4	Lavender
5	Roses
18	Yarrow
1	Hemlock

Regional plant alternatives on pages 119-123. For suggested fertilizers, see page 97.

15 ft.

22 ft.

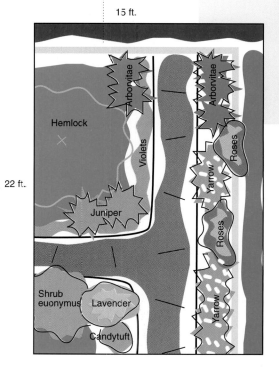

Q: The walkway along the side of our house is cut off from our side yard by a solid wall of shrubbery that gives the spot a gloomy air. How can we give the area a more open feeling, and improve the view from inside our house?

LOCATION
Side Yard

A: Though it's hard for many gardeners to do, sometimes they must get rid of mature plants in order to make space for new ones. Your best bet may be to dig up that dreary hedge, clearing the way for sunshine, and replace the plants with a broad border of flowering perennials and annuals. The views from both your house and your yard will improve.

Design the bed around five or six flowering shrubs, such as roses, to provide structure. Though people often think of isolating roses in their own separate plot, many rose varieties thrive when surrounded by other plants, and continuous-bloomers, such as floribundas, will provide color throughout the summer months. Other star performers for such a spot include heartleaf crambe, which provides a generous cloud of airy white blossoms much like baby's breath, and artemisia, with its feathery silver foliage. For low mounds of color, include cranesbill geraniums, a perennial with delicate, five-lobed flowers. Across from the bed, frame one of the windows in your home with a leafy porcelain ampelopsis vine growing up a trellis.

WHAT YOU NEED:

REGION
A **B** C

Plants for Region B

4	Foxglove
3	Delphiniums
12	Roses
5	Irises
3	Artemisia
1	Porcelain ampelopsis
4	Canterbury bells
2	Heartleaf crambe
2	Cranesbill geraniums
3	Allium
4	Miniature roses

Regional plant alternatives on pages 119-123. For suggested fertilizers, see page 97.

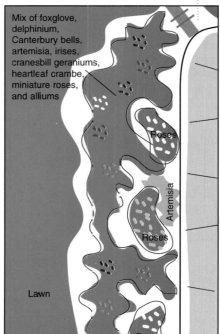

36 ft.

Mix of foxglove, delphinium, Canterbury bells, artemisia, irises, cranesbill geraniums, heartleaf crambe, miniature roses, and alliums

58 ft.

Roses

Artemisia

Roses

Lawn

Roses

Q: I'm eager to give my yard a more exuberant, cheerful look, but I don't have the patience to wait the months it takes for a garden to fill in and flower. What's the quickest way to add lots of color and impact to my yard?

Take a cue from your Victorian predecessors and make use of annual bedding plants, such as wax begonia and New Guinea impatiens, planted in mass. Although they won't provide profuse blooms overnight, within a month they'll fill in and offer a display of color visitors to your home won't soon forget.

If you're really in a hurry, buy annuals in 4-inch pots and sink the pots directly into the ground. Plants toward the back of a bed can even be set on top of the soil; the plants at the front will camouflage the containers. For flowers that will last for months, however, it's best to give your plants a stable home. Most annuals prefer rich, moist soil, so incorporate plenty of organic matter before you plant, and water plants well during the hot summer months. Lovers of annuals provide this tip: Since many bedding plants are low-growers, plants toward the back of the bed can sometimes be lost to view. For the best display, slope the soil up at the back of your planting bed.

WHAT YOU NEED:

REGION
A B C

Plants for Regions B & C

90	Wax begonias
15	Impatiens
20	New Guinea impatiens
12	Geraniums
70	Marigolds
45	Hiemalis begonias
24	Boxwoods

Regional plant alternatives on pages 119-123. For suggested fertilizers, see page 97.

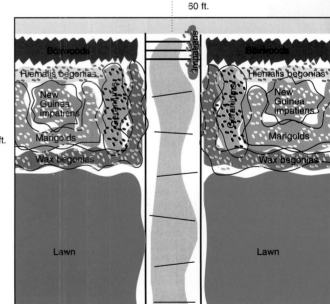

Q: We'd enjoy having a luxurious garden at our small summer house, but would rather spend our vacation time with book or fishing pole in hand than trowel and clippers. What can we plant that will take care of itself?

A: Try carpeting the ground around your cottage with daylilies, one of the least demanding of all perennials and a longtime garden favorite. These hardy plants care little about soil type or climate all they demand is ample water during their blooming period.

If you like, include a variety of types (daylilies range from 1 foot to more than 4 feet in height and are available in warm colors from deep mahogany to salmon pink). To ensure bloom from late spring into fall, mix early, mid-season, and late-blooming varieties. Or, rely on the 'Stella d'Oro' daylily, which offers up golden yellow blooms all summer long. Some daylilies will retain their leaves year round; if your summer cottage is in a mild-winter climate, you might want to concentrate on these evergreen types. Plants that mingle well with daylilies and provide additional color punch include spiky purple liatris and black-eyed Susans (rudbeckia). All make excellent cut flowers, too.

WHAT YOU NEED:

REGION

A   B   C

Plants for Regions A, B, & C

60 Daylilies
 1 Deciduous magnolia
15 Black-eyed Susans
 8 Liatris

Regional plant alternatives on pages 119-123. For suggested fertilizers, see page 97.

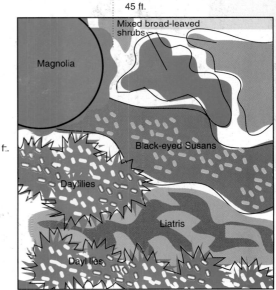

45 ft.

Mixed broad-leaved shrubs

Magnolia

55 ft.

Black-eyed Susans

Daylilies

Liatris

Daylilies

Q: The winters in our part of the country are so cold and dreary that by spring I'm ready for an explosion of color in the yard. I love bulbs, but my plantings always look kind of sparse. What am I doing wrong?

A: You're on the right track; bulbs are one of the best ways to ensure vivid color in the garden from early spring on into summer. But perhaps you're being too timid in your approach. Many people buy a handful of tulip or daffodil bulbs, then spread them throughout the yard. For the most impact, however, bulbs should be massed together. (For more information on planting bulbs, see pages 110-111.)

But bulbs alone are not enough. To avoid having your tulips and hyacinths look like soldiers lined up for review, partially fill your planting bed with low-mounding plants, such as juniper, euonymus, or blue fescue, a decorative grass. Include other spring-blooming flowers, such as violas or candytuft. Then fill the pockets in between with clusters of identical bulbs, preferably no fewer than 12 in number, spaced from 5 to 8 inches apart. For the fullest burst of color, pick bulbs with similar bloom periods. Otherwise, include early, mid-season, and late-blooming types to extend your spring display.

WHAT YOU NEED:

REGION

A B C

Plants for Regions A & B

1	Crab apple tree
1	Juniper tree
3	Euonymus
24	Daffodils
3	Dusty millers
20	Hyacinths
5	Blue fescues
200	Tulips
10	Pansies
3	Candytufts

Regional plant alternatives on pages 119-123. For suggested fertilizers, see page 97.

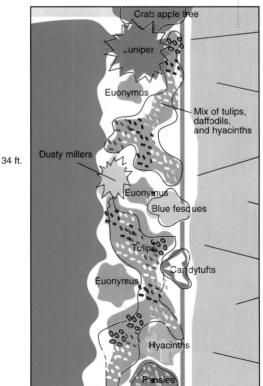

20 ft.

Crab apple tree

Juniper

Euonymus

Mix of tulips, daffodils, and hyacinths

34 ft.   Dusty millers

Euonymus

Blue fescues

Tulips

Candytufts

Euonymus

Hyacinths

Pansies

Q: The garden bed I see from my kitchen window looks great in early summer, but quickly fades to green (or brown) thereafter. How can I extend the blooming period so that I can enjoy flowers throughout the growing season?

A: It takes careful planning to have continual color in any garden bed, but the rewards are well worth the trouble. Before planting in the spring, study bloom seasons carefully, and choose some plants, such as yarrow or low-growing erodium, that will flower continuously from early summer into fall. Another way to ensure a lengthy bloom period is to start some flowers, such as Shirley poppy, from seed sown at intervals from spring through summer.

Intermix other plants, either seeded or from nursery transplants, according to their season of primary bloom. Toadflax (linaria), campanula, and baby's breath, for instance, will put on their best display in early summer, while scarlet flax, dwarf globe amaranth, and annual phlox will bloom through the late-summer months. If you also plant coreopsis and annual salvia, they will take over and lend their Indian-summer hues in the early fall. A bonus: Many of these plants will reseed, ensuring another multi-season display next year.

WHAT YOU NEED:

REGION
A   B   C

Plants for Regions A, B, & C

9	Scarlet flax
13	Poppies
10	Toadflax
3	Erodium
10	Dwarf globe amaranth
5	Yarrow
6	Campanula
10	Baby's breath
6	Annual phlox
10	Tickseed
12	Catchflies

Regional plant alternatives on pages 119-123. For suggested fertilizers, see page 97.

15 ft.

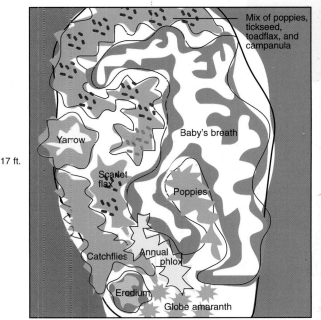

17 ft.

Mix of poppies, tickseed, toadflax, and campanula

Yarrow

Baby's breath

Scarlet flax

Poppies

Catchflies

Annual phlox

Erodium

Globe amaranth

Background photo, left: Campanula and baby's breath bloom best in early summer. Left inset: Coreopsis and salvia add color in early fall. Right inset: Shirley poppies bloom red in late summer.

Q: **We have plenty of flowers blooming throughout the peak of summer, but by the time the first hint of fall is in the air, most of the glory is gone. How can we pump up our garden beds to match the season's brilliant foliage?**

A: Put on your own fall show by focusing at least one garden bed on late-bloomers, which display their finest hues just as the gardening season is coming to a frosty end.

Annuals, such as chrysanthemum and lavender-blue ageratum, will provide bright bursts of color throughout the fall. But for dazzling blooms in exceptional hues, give dahlias a try. These flowers sprout from tuberous roots and rise to heights topping 6 feet, yet there are many bush and dwarf forms perfect for lower garden beds. After the soil has warmed in the spring, set tubers flat in 4-inch-deep planting holes. (Dahlias prefer rich, well-drained soil.) Keep plants moist while blooming, from summer through killing frosts, then cut back plants and carefully dig up tubers. Let dry for a few hours, and store through the winter in sand, dry peat moss, or vermiculite. In spring, cut tubers apart, retaining at least one growing shoot in each clump, and replant. You also can start dwarf dahlias from seed.

WHAT YOU NEED:

REGION

A B C

Plants for Region A

10 **Dahlias**
7 **Marguerite daisies**
14 **Mums**
50 **Ageratum**

Regional plant alternatives on pages 119-123. For suggested fertilizers, see page 97.

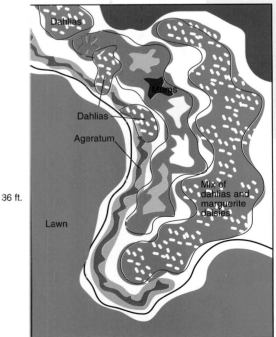

26 ft.

36 ft.

Dahlias

Mums

Dahlias

Ageratum

Mix of dahlias and marguerite daisies

Lawn

Q: I'm tired of setting out plants that bloom gloriously for one or two months but then quickly go downhill. Isn't there some way I can have flowers for more of the year without putting in a lot more work?

14 SEASONAL COLOR
Three Seasons

A: Not only can you have bright blossoms for three seasons of the year, but if you include hardy perennials in your planting and prepare your soil well, the glory will be repeated year after year.

Many perennials bloom for only a few weeks at a time, and the beds they're in require careful planning in order to maintain color throughout the growing season. But a few perennials will give you color from late spring all the way into fall, particularly if you remove spent flowers to encourage repeat blossoming. Two such prolific performers are campanula and coreopsis, both of which have low- and medium-size forms that work well at the front or middle of a flower border. Choose tall-growers, such as malva or purple loosestrife, to bring up the rear; in between, mix various kinds of roses. For longest and fullest bloom, choose polyantha or floribunda rose types.

WHAT YOU NEED:

REGION
A B C

Plants for Regions A, B, & C

- 6 Roses
- 4 Loosestrife
- 7 Cosmos
- 3 Celosia
- 1 Geranium
- 3 Lobelia
- 3 Coreopsis
- 15 Campanula
- 5 Marigolds
- 1 Lavender

Regional plant alternatives on pages 119-123. For suggested fertilizers, see page 97.

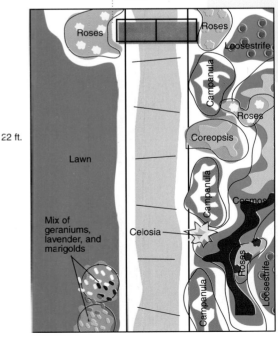

STYLE OF GARDEN
Perennial Border

Q: I've always grown annual flowers, such as zinnias and petunias, but I'm bored with their orderly look. Yet perennials have always seemed a bit intimidating. What's a good way to get my feet wet in the perennial world?

A: Set aside one wide garden bed in your yard this year and devote it entirely to perennials. Remember, though, that these long-lived plants are slow growers compared with annuals. Have patience and you'll soon be rewarded.

In mild-winter areas, prepare the soil and plant the bed in the fall, before cold weather sets in. Winter rains will help the new plants establish healthy root systems, ready to support vigorous growth come spring. In cold-winter areas, plant in early spring. Choose a wide variety of plants, and arrange loosely according to height— low plants in the front and tall plants in the back. Stagger plants rather than planting in rows to avoid a rigid look. See what thrives. Discover what you like. Observe what plant pairs complement one another. Then next fall, rearrange plants and plant new beds based on lessons learned; most perennials can be moved without harm.

WHAT YOU NEED:

REGION A B C

Plants for Regions A & B

- 7 Loosestrife
- 4 Daylilies
- 3 Daisies
- 8 Coreopsis
- 5 Phlox
- 9 Pearly everlastings (*Anaphalis margaritacea*)
- 8 Goldenrods
- 3 Primroses
- 5 Hollyhock mallow
- 6 Monarda (bee balm)
- 1 Clematis

Regional plant alternatives on pages 119-123. For suggested fertilizers, see page 97.

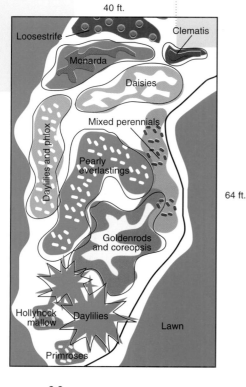

40 ft.

Loosestrife

Clematis

Monarda

Daisies

Mixed perennials

Daylilies and phlox

Pearly everlastings

64 ft.

Goldenrods and coreopsis

Hollyhock mallow

Daylilies

Lawn

Primroses

Q: The junipers that surround our yard provide wind protection and privacy, but are a bit dreary for our tastes. How can we brighten up the yard without spending all of our summer slaving in the garden?

A: Once established, a bed of hardy perennials will serve up month after month of color, all with little effort on your part. To get plants off to a good start, prepare soil by working in organic matter to help retain water and provide nutrients, along with coarse sand to promote drainage if the soil is particularly heavy.

To minimize the oppressive darkness of your evergreen backdrop, plan your garden bed around mounds of tall-growing perennials in a range of sunny colors. Yarrow, monarda (bee balm), perennial sunflowers, and phlox all will quickly fill in the front of the bed, while spiked specimens, such as rocket ligularia, bugbane (cimicifuga), and campanula, will shoot skyward at the rear. You might fill in with purple coneflower, gaillardia, and Shasta daisy. Remove spent blooms and keep plants well watered during the hot summer months, and the border will reward you with color well into the fall.

WHAT YOU NEED:

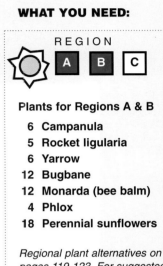

REGION

A   B   C

Plants for Regions A & B

  6 Campanula
  5 Rocket ligularia
  6 Yarrow
12 Bugbane
12 Monarda (bee balm)
  4 Phlox
18 Perennial sunflowers

Regional plant alternatives on pages 119-123. For suggested fertilizers, see page 97.

15 ft.

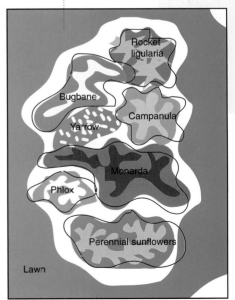

20 ft.

Q: We love the bright swaths of color that annuals provide, but our soil is far from rich. And, it's hard for us to find time for setting out bedding plants. Can we still get some of the rewards of an annual border without all the work?

A: The answer is yes, if you're willing to let nature and the seasons give you a hand. The key is to choose plants that will overwinter, or that will go to seed, sprout next season, and grow again under the conditions you've described.

Your time will be well invested if you work at least a small amount of organic matter into the soil to help retain moisture between waterings. Then choose a few easy-care, year-round growers, such as geranium or ice plant, to give the bed a permanent structure. Mix in broad clumps of hardy annuals, such as baby marguerite daisies, by sowing seeds in place or transplanting nursery plants. You may want to fill in with annuals that are prone to reseeding, such as California poppy, linaria, Mexican evening primrose, Johnny jump-up, clarkia, love-in-a-mist, sweet alyssum, and statice. Pull up plants after they've gone to seed. Larkspur may not reseed readily, but you can sow seeds in place each fall for bloom the next year.

WHAT YOU NEED:

REGION

A B **C**

Plants for Region C

1	New Zealand tea tree
3	Geraniums
24	Baby marguerite daisies
6	Ice plants
4	Climbing roses
24	Poppies

Regional plant alternatives on pages 119-123. For suggested fertilizers, see page 97.

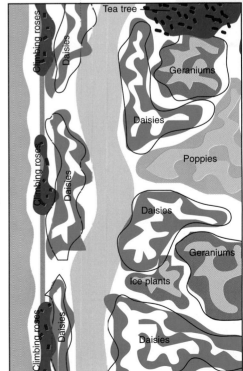

18 STYLE OF GARDEN
Mixed Border

Q: We spend a lot of time in our back yard during the summer and enjoy our lush lawn. But we'd love to have more flowers to look at. What kinds can we plant that will brighten the summer months?

A: If you limit your plantings to a carefully planned border, you can preserve most of your lawn space and still have ample room for both annuals and perennials to shine.

While a flower border can be planned to take up minimum space, allow 5 feet or more for the width of the bed if you have room to spread out. A curving border will set off the beauty of your lawn; establish the outline of the bed with a garden hose before beginning to remove the sod. Then choose plants that fit into three different height zones, such as petunia, marigold, and dwarf snapdragon, for the low-edge zone along the front; zinnia, artemisia, marguerite, snapdragon, and black-eyed Susans for the mid-height zone; and delphinium, loosestrife, and garden phlox for the tall zone at the back of the bed. Some of these flowers occasionally suffer from powdery mildew or rust; minimize problems by soaking the soil when you water rather than sprinkling from overhead.

WHAT YOU NEED:

REGION
A B C

Plants for Regions A & B

20	Petunias
4	Golden marguerites
10	Phlox
5	Black-eyed Susans
6	Snapdragons
6	Zinnias
9	Loosestrife
8	Larkspur
4	Artemisia
16	French marigolds
3	Rhododendron
15	Ageratum

Regional plant alternatives on pages 119-123. For suggested fertilizers, see page 97.

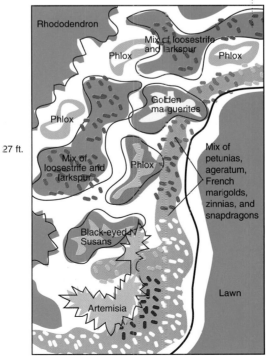

18 ft.

Rhododendron

Mix of loosestrife and larkspur

Phlox

Phlox

27 ft.

Phlox

Golden marguerites

Mix of loosestrife and larkspur

Phlox

Mix of petunias, ageratum, French marigolds, zinnias, and snapdragons

Black-eyed Susans

Lawn

Artemisia

Q: I've always loved the look of an old-fashioned cottage garden with lots of spring bulbs and summer perennials, and think it would suit my old farmhouse. But what can I plant that will bridge the gap between daffodils and daisies?

A: For many cottage gardeners, it's the second wave of spring bloom that provides the most pleasure of all. Blooming from mid-spring into early summer are lush flowers with rich fragrance that would fade in summer's heat but that tantalize the senses during this transitional season.

Gardeners who live in mild- and cold-winter climes are particularly blessed; they're able to enjoy two of the cottage garden's most charming mid-season occupants. Peonies, for instance, provide an embarrassment of riches: huge, sweet-scented blossoms, mounds of deep green foliage, and years of beauty. Bleeding heart also will thrive, planted in the shade of the peonies. Like their sun-loving mates, these romantic plants with their arching stems of rose-pink hearts will return to charm each spring. Other prized performers include the ornamental onion (allium, which is planted as a bulb in the fall), many of which are sweetly scented and bloom through summer. All of these classic plants make excellent cut flowers.

WHAT YOU NEED:

REGION

A B C

Plants for Regions A & B

  1 **Arborvitae**
  2 **Juniper**
  3 **Potentilla**
16 **Ornamental onions**
  4 **Lamb's ears**
  4 **Foxglove**
  7 **Irises**
  5 **Peonies**
  2 **Bleeding hearts**

Regional plant alternatives on pages 119-123. For suggested fertilizers, see page 97.

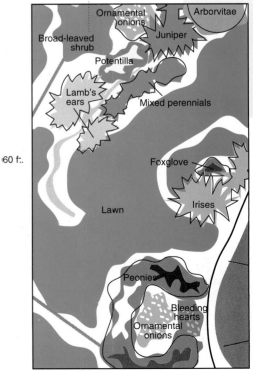

40 ft.

60 ft.

Q: My memories of my grandmother's garden include an untamed tangle of flowers alive with fascinating creatures, from butterflies and ladybugs to hummingbirds and caterpillars. How can I attract these insects and wildlife to my yard?

A: Serve up a tasty smorgasbord of favored perennial flowers, and wildlife will flock to your yard throughout the blooming season. Although any brightly colored, nectar-rich flower will bring some curious birds and insects, a few flower varieties are guaranteed to attract a horde of friendly visitors. For best results, plant a wide garden border with staggered masses of flowers, such as daylily, butterfly flower, liatris, purple loosestrife, and Queen Anne's lace. Other tasty choices for the chow line include helianthus, coneflower, yarrow, bee balm, and tigerlily, along with lantana, fuchsia, lavender, and columbine. To attract as many visitors as possible, try to avoid using insecticides in this area.

Along with masses of bright flowers, be sure to include a shallow birdbath as well as a sturdy bird feeder, mounted where scattered seed won't wreak havoc with your established plants and lawn. Lastly, place a comfortable garden bench in a strategic spot and settle in to enjoy the mealtime show.

WHAT YOU NEED:

REGION
A B C

Plants for Regions A, B, & C

30 Loosestrife
18 Yarrow
30 Daylilies
 5 Liatris
15 Pansies
 8 Queen Anne's lace

Regional plant alternatives on pages 119-123. For suggested fertilizers, see page 97.

32 ft.

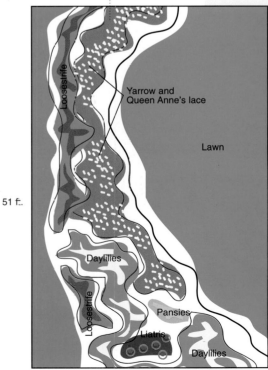

51 ft.

Q: My wife and I enjoy traditional and formal garden styles, and have loved touring many stately European and American gardens as a result. How can we incorporate that timeless look here at home on a reasonable scale?

A: With their strict geometry and manicured boxwood or germander edgings, traditional herb gardens are among horticulture's most formal expressions. Yet their functionality makes them far from stuffy or sterile; in a well-planned herb garden, there are pleasures for the senses at every turn.

A variety of planting designs is possible, from segmented circles to a square within a square, depending on the size of your plot. After you've determined your design on paper, transfer it to the garden, edging all beds with brick, stone, or pressure-treated lumber. Add sand and organic matter as needed to ensure good drainage. Group plants according to watering needs, and place similar plants symmetrically to achieve a balanced, formal look. Don't be afraid to include nonherbal plants; roses, espaliered fruit trees, and scented plants, such as heliotrope, all magnify an herb garden's many charms.

WHAT YOU NEED:

REGION

| A | **B** | **C** |

Plants for Regions B & C

- 2 Lavender
- 2 Lavender cotton (grey santolina)
- 44 Boxwoods
- 3 Roses
- 1 Lovage
- 3 Nepeta
- 4 Feverfew
- 8 Signet marigolds

Regional plant alternatives on pages 119-123. For suggested fertilizers, see page 97.

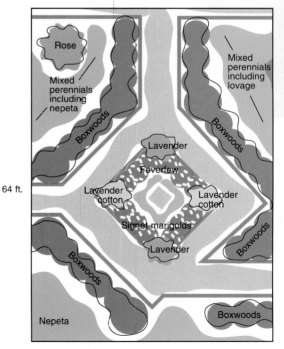

Q: On drives in the country when I was a child, we used to see great meadows full of beautiful flowers. I loved the way they looked, and still prefer that wild feeling to more formal gardens. How can I create that casual look at home?

A: Choose an open sunny spot, spread seeds with abandon, and you can re-create those unstudied floral scenes from your childhood. But before taking on the role of Mother Nature, prepare your plot by digging in organic matter and sand if the soil is mostly clay. Water the area well and wait for weeds to sprout, then hoe them down. The more weeds you remove at this stage, the easier your long-term maintenance job will be.

Sow seeds as soon as the soil warms in the spring; in a warm climate, many annuals also can be sown in the fall for spring bloom. For a natural look, plant great drifts of a single flower type, such as old-fashioned-looking annual daisies. Once seedlings sprout, thin to allow 8 to 12 inches between plants. If desired, sow wildflower seeds, such as California poppy, lupine, and columbine for additional color; along shady margins, cineraria grows well.

WHAT YOU NEED:

REGION

A B **C**

Plants for Region C

3	Lavender
1	Palm
86	Daisies
5	Cineraria
3	Delphiniums
12	California poppies
1	Fuchsia
4	Climbing roses
6	Daylilies

Regional plant alternatives on pages 119-123. For suggested fertilizers, see page 97.

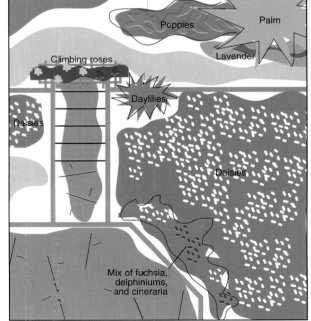

Q: Our Victorian-era home sits on a large lot with little but lawn and trees to enhance it. We'd like to create a prettier setting, but we're a bit overwhelmed by the amount of work involved. We'd like something that would eventually almost take care of itself. Where should we start?

A: Don't feel you have to replant your entire yard. Instead, hold onto a good portion of your established lawn, and concentrate on replanting areas where your efforts will be most appreciated—those closest to sidewalks, pathways, or your front door—with plants that naturalize, or reproduce and spread. To keep from getting burned out, break the work of preparing the soil and planting new plants into weekend-size chunks, tackling no more than a 10-by-10-foot section at a time.

To minimize future gardening chores and establish an old-fashioned look, fill each new section of your garden with perennial plants, such as purple coneflower, canna lily, or lantana, that essentially care for themselves. Include a preponderance of daylilies; clumps of these time-honored favorites will grow bigger every year. For summer-long color, include varieties that are early-, mid-, and late-season bloomers. Daylilies can be divided if desired, but also will flourish if left untouched.

WHAT YOU NEED:

REGION
A B C

Plants for Regions A, B, & C

  6 **Lantana**
80 **Daylilies**
20 **Dwarf daylilies**
  6 **Purple coneflowers**
36 **Violas**
  6 **Miniature roses**
100 **Liriope**
12 **Golden marguerites**
  9 **Lily-of-the-Nile**

Regional plant alternatives on pages 119-123. For suggested fertilizers, see page 97.

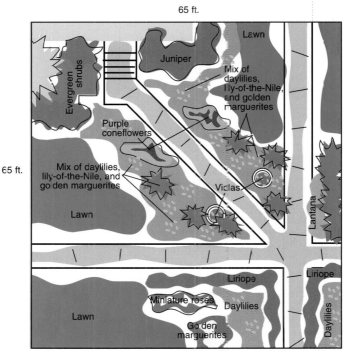

65 ft.

65 ft.

Lawn

Juniper

Evergreen shrubs

Mix of daylilies, lily-of-the-Nile, and golden marguerites

Purple coneflowers

Mix of daylilies, lily-of-the-Nile, and golden marguerites

Lawn

Violas

Lantana

Lawn

Liriope

Liriope

Miniature roses

Daylilies

Daylilies

Lawn

Golden marguerites

Q: Now that our kids are grown and gone, we no longer need so much lawn space in our back yard. We also have more time for gardening, and would love to fill the yard with soft color and fragrance. Any ideas?

A: While most flower gardens take advantage of a yard's perimeters, leaving a lake of grass in the middle, the reverse of that tactic would work well for you. By placing a broad island of flowers in the middle of your lawn, you can enjoy them—and tend them—from all angles.

Define the outline of your island with a garden hose or rope, then remove sod from inside the boundaries. Amend with organic matter and sand as needed to produce a light, rich, fast-draining soil. Scotts® 3-in-1 Organic Mix is perfect. Give height to the center of the island with a mountain range of roses and foxglove in soft shades of pink, white, and dusty red. For maximum fragrance, look for old-fashioned, highly scented rose varieties. (See pages 106-109 for tips on growing roses.) Provide rolling foothills with baby marguerite daisies and richly scented stock, then include a mix of cool-colored annuals and perennials along the shoreline: blue marguerite, sweet william, spicy carnation, sweet alyssum, and English daisy.

WHAT YOU NEED:

REGION

A B **C**

Plants for Region C

9	Roses
12	Foxglove
36	Sweet alyssum
6	English daisies
5	Sweet williams
9	Annual phlox
8	Daisies
8	Stock
3	Blue marguerites
6	Carnations
9	Lavender

Regional plant alternatives on pages 119-123. For suggested fertilizers, see page 97.

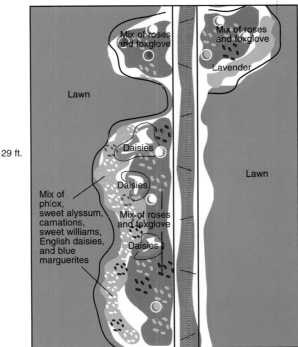

22 ft.

29 ft.

Mix of roses and foxglove

Mix of roses and foxglove

Lavender

Lawn

Lawn

Daisies

Daisies

Mix of phlox, sweet alyssum, carnations, sweet williams, English daisies, and blue marguerites

Mix of roses and foxglove

Daisies

Q: I know that gardens in small spaces are supposed to be restrained and in scale with their surroundings. But I live in the middle of the city, and I'd rather relax in more exuberant surroundings. How can I foster that feeling?

A: Rules, as they say, are made to be broken. There's no reason, for instance, that you can't have a slice of wild prairie in your tiny yard—a mad tangle of hardy flowers that surrounds you with nature's glory.

Begin by digging plenty of nutrient-rich organic matter into your garden beds, if needed; even native flowers like to get off to a good start. Scotts® 3-in-1 Organic Mix is a rich mixture of organic materials. Then, rather than heeding standard advice about placing low plants in the front of your garden beds and tall specimens in the back, intermix wild-looking perennial plants, such as lythrum, veronica, phlox, purple coneflower, monarda, and yarrow. For a wealth of blooms, sow larkspur seeds in patches throughout the garden in the fall and again in early spring. To extend the bloom period, pull up larkspur once the flowers fade (save the seeds for planting later) and replace with summer annuals, such as blue salvia, snapdragon, or nicotiana. To avoid complete chaos, limit your color choices to a few cool hues.

WHAT YOU NEED:

REGION

A   B   C

Plants for Region C

18 **Larkspur**
6 **Purple coneflowers**
2 **Phlox**
4 **Veronica**
2 **Cape plumbago**
1 **Clematis**

Regional plant alternatives on pages 119-123. For suggested fertilizers, see page 97.

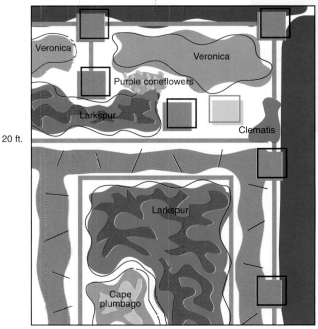

18 ft.

20 ft.

Q: Our small, walled-in yard must play multiple roles as garden, living space, and inviting entry for guests. How can I keep the space from feeling too crowded, yet still give it the welcoming feeling I want?

A: Though your space is small, it's still possible to divide and conquer. Contrary to conventional wisdom, sometimes breaking an area into smaller units and using a variety of surfacing materials can make it seem larger.

Since your yard must lead visitors from your front gate to your front door, begin there. Make plans for a concrete, brick, or stone pathway at least 3 feet across, and flank it with planting beds of equal width, edged with river rock. At the same time, set aside an area for a cozy patio to the side of one of the planting beds; bricks or flagstones set in sand make for an easy-care surface that drains well when it rains. At the nursery, choose plants that have a low, mounding, or spreading growth habit so that the garden areas have a predominantly horizontal feel to enhance the illusion of space. In areas too tight for planting beds, add extra color and texture with window boxes or potted annuals, such as petunias or zinnias.

WHAT YOU NEED:

REGION
A B C

Plants for Regions A, B, & C

1	Silver lace vine
3	Pink geraniums
4	Scaevola
3	Double petunias
9	Petunias
5	*Delphinium belladonna*
8	Shasta daisies
3	Dusty miller
6	Zinnias
4	Coreopsis
8	Lupine
3	Lavender
30	Hen-and-chickens

Regional plant alternatives on pages 119-123. For suggested fertilizers, see page 97.

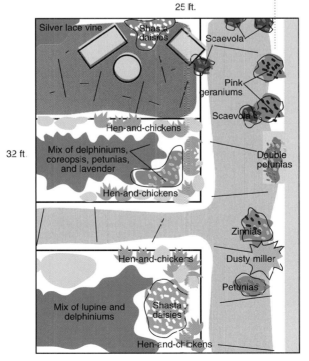

Q: Our back yard is large but boring, with grass from edge to edge and little of interest other than a single shade tree. We'd like to create a more lush, intimate space with lots of color. Where do we begin?

A: Soften the squareness of your yard by marking out deep, sinuous planting beds with a rope or garden hose. Don't be afraid to include plenty of curves; they'll help break up the large space and give it a cozier feel. Once you're satisfied with the layout of the beds, remove the sod, turn the soil, and add organic material as necessary. (For a yard this large, you might want to prepare and plant the beds in stages, dividing them into manageable sections.)

Anchor the beds visually by planting tall, shrubby plants, such as long-blooming floribunda roses, along the fence line. Then fill in the beds with plants of descending height. Include a preponderance of hardy perennials, such as purple coneflower and campanula, along with more short-lived but colorful specimens, such as delphinium, poppy, and lupine. For best effect, mix plant shapes (spiky, mounding, upright, horizontal) and repeat favorite combinations at intervals throughout the border.

WHAT YOU NEED:

REGION
A B C

Plants for Regions A & B

- 3 **Delphinium**
- 15 **Foxglove**
- 6 **Floribunda roses**
- 3 **Purple coneflowers**
- 9 **Poppies**
- 3 **Lupine**
- 2 **Yarrow**
- 2 **Campanula**
- 2 **Arborvitae**

Regional plant alternatives on pages 119-123. For suggested fertilizers, see page 97.

45 ft.

Climbing roses

Floribunda roses

Mix of purple coneflower and campanula

Delphinium

Arborvitae

Poppies

32 ft.

Lupine

Foxglove

Lawn

Yarrow

Foxglove

Q: We would like to have the color and grace of a traditional perennial border in our yard, but our mountain summers are short, and the winters harsh. Many of the plants we've tried don't survive at this altitude. Any suggestions?

A: Mountain areas are notorious for being short on topsoil, and what soil there is often is short on organic matter. Bring in supplementary soil, if necessary, and prepare planting beds by incorporating plenty of organic material. Scotts® Flower Planting Soil provides a rich mixture of organic materials in the fall for planting the following spring. If possible, choose a protected, south-facing site so the soil will warm faster once the snow recedes.

Besides soil preparation, the key to a successful mountain garden lies in picking plants that not only will endure the long, cold winters, but that actually prefer such conditions. Many hardy perennials make suitable high-altitude substitutes for more tender traditional plants; some best-suited to mountain climes include astilbe, monarda (bee balm), Shasta daisy, and summer phlox. For winter protection, cover beds with a thick blanket of mulch after plants die back in the fall prior to the first frost.

WHAT YOU NEED:

REGION

A B C

Plants for Regions A & B

- 1 Colorado blue spruce
- 6 Monarda (bee balm)
- 3 Shasta daisies
- 9 Cleome
- 10 Foxglove
- 4 Summer phlox
- 5 Astilbe
- 6 Strawflowers
- 2 Azaleas
- 2 Daylilies

Regional plant alternatives on pages 119-123. For suggested fertilizers, see page 97.

30 ft.

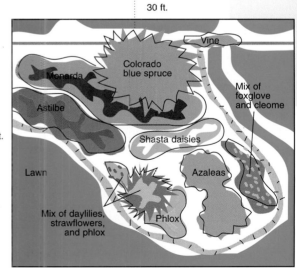

27 ft.

Q: The entryway to our home is flanked by a dry, barren slope that tends to erode during our winter rains. We'd like something more colorful to greet our guests, but don't have a lot of time to fuss. What might flourish in this spot?

A: First, terrace that slope with low stone walls to provide a foothold for plants and prevent further erosion. Use the largest rocks at the base of the walls and smaller rocks at the top. Slant the walls slightly inward against the slope for stability. As you build the beds, backfill them with good garden soil. To promote drainage, do not mortar the rocks in place.

When beds are prepared, set up a background for colorful flowers by choosing evergreen shrubs or groundcovers known for their easy-care nature, such as grevillea, mock orange, or forget-me-not. Pick out low-growing varieties in scale with the walls. Then create pockets of color in between foliage plants with flowering annuals or perennials. Some favorites, such as petunias, may require more moisture than other plants; add organic matter when planting to compensate. Succulent, rock-garden-type plants, such as sedum or echeveria, add year-round color and texture and require little care or water.

WHAT YOU NEED:

REGION

A   B   **C**

Plants for Region C

 3 **Mock oranges**
 1 **Grevillea**
12 **Petunias**
 5 **Forget-me-nots**
 6 **Pink marguerites**
10 **Columbines**
15 **Sedum and
     mixed succulents**
 4 **Foxglove**

Regional plant alternatives on pages 119-123. For suggested fertilizers, see page 97.

34 ft.

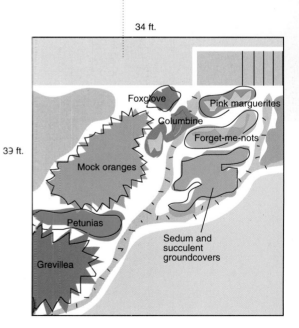

WHAT YOU NEED:

REGION

A B C

Plants for Regions B & C

- 2 Red hot pokers
- 3 Hollyhocks
- 4 Roses
- 7 Perennial flax
- 3 Yarrow

Regional plant alternatives on pages 119-123. For suggested fertilizers, see page 97.

16 ft.

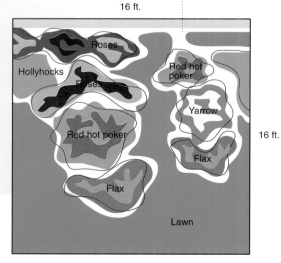

16 ft.

Q: I love having an array of summer flowers in my yard, but nothing seems to thrive in the poor, dry soil. Short of replacing the soil and starting over, how can I achieve the bright, full look I want?

A: Avoid a lot of back-breaking work by choosing plants already adapted to poor soil and droughtlike conditions. Many native plants from California, the Southwest, Australia, and South Africa will take readily to such an inhospitable home once they're established by a season of regular watering.

Exotic plants, such as red hot poker, favored by many Victorian-era gardeners, provide great mounds of vibrant color with little care; the torchlike flower spikes also attract hummingbirds. Mix with other drought-tolerant stars, such as perennial flax (which naturalizes easily) or yarrow. Once the bulk of your plantings are in place, allow yourself a few choosier plants, such as hollyhocks or a floribunda rose or two. Dig in plenty of organic matter just where the plants' roots will go; follow up after planting with a thick layer of organic mulch.

Q: The soil around my house isn't the greatest; it's more like sand than soil, actually. My lawn does fine, but I'd like to grow something more interesting. Are there plants that like these kinds of conditions?

A: Herbs are among the easiest and most rewarding plants to grow, and actually prefer the sandy soil type you've described. If your soil has little or no organic matter, however, it would be best to amend it with organic material or even with commercial planting mix if the area is small. Scotts® Planting Soil is a rich blend of nutrients perfect for planting herbs.

Many gardeners arrange their herbs in formally patterned beds. But among the most effective ways to display these low, multitextured plants is tucking them among a variety of rocks or letting them creep between flagstones. (Other gardeners may be ridding their planting beds of rocks; keep a sharp eye out for freebies while walking or driving through your neighborhood.) If cooking isn't your forte, don't despair; herbs such as lamb's ear, tricolor sage, or signet marigold are grown primarily for their color, foliage texture, or flowers.

WHAT YOU NEED:

REGION   A   B   C

Plants for Regions A, B, & C

6	Turtlehead
6	Tricolor sages
2	Santolina
10	Signet marigolds
6	Lamb's ears
6	Lavender
1	Tansy

Regional plant alternatives on pages 119-123. For suggested fertilizers, see page 97.

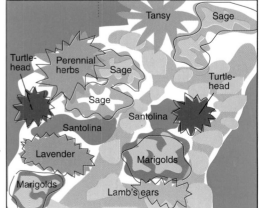

Q: The planting bed along our driveway gets little water and bakes in the sun that reflects from an adjacent stucco wall. What can we plant that will provide color and texture but won't shrivel in the intense heat or die from thirst?

A: Don't fight what nature has given you. Instead, surrender to the elements and choose plants native to the Southwest or other areas that endure searing summer heat and little annual rainfall. All love fast-draining, sandy soil.

Though your planting site is narrow, you've still got room for layering plants of various heights. First, cut back on the heat reflected from your stucco wall by lining up a battery of tall, sun-loving desert natives, such as organ-pipe cactus, palmlike agave, and succulent aloe. (Too much water will kill some of these plants far sooner than not enough.) Position shorter cacti or succulent varieties in front, mixed with colorful perennial sea lavender, which puts forth papery purple blooms throughout the summer season. Finally, for a particularly brilliant border, include ice plant along the driveway's edge; its intense colors hold up well in the desert sun. Yellow, orange, hot pink, purple, and red varieties all are available.

WHAT YOU NEED:

REGION

A B **C**

Plants for Region C

2 **Organ-pipe cacti**
5 **Sea lavender**
36 **Ice plants**
4 **Agave**
2 **Aloes**

Organ-pipe cacti grow only in parts of Region C. Regional plant alternatives for the other plants on pages 119-123. For suggested fertilizers, see page 97.

42 ft.

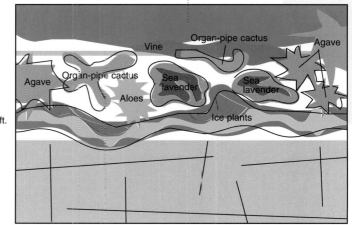

27 ft.

LOCATION
Front Entry

Q: Visitors arrive at our lightly shaded doorway via a beautiful brick pathway, but with nothing but lawn on either side, the walk looks rather bare and uninviting. How can we dress it up and tie it to the rest of the yard?

A: Front entries often are neglected while foundation plantings get all the attention. Yet, as the first thing visitors see, a well-landscaped walkway can set the tone for an entire yard.

Establish planting beds along the sidewalk in front of the house, and curve them to continue along your walkway. Make beds a minimum of 3 feet in width; a narrower planting may look spindly and won't provide room for massed flowers. Choose two or three plant varieties to provide the backbone of the beds. They should serve double duty, providing both evergreen foliage and seasonal flowers. Bergenia, star jasmine, and lily-of-the-Nile do well on both counts; lily-of-the-Nile also provides a vertical accent. Where the sun shines for part of the day, edge the walkway with annuals, such as petunia, marigold, or sweet alyssum. In sections of the bed that receive the most shade, fill in with impatiens, lobelia, English daisy, or primrose.

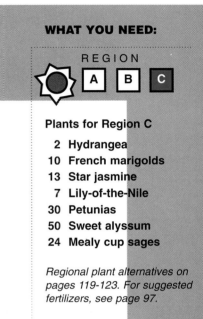

WHAT YOU NEED:

REGION

A B **C**

Plants for Region C

2	Hydrangea
10	French marigolds
13	Star jasmine
7	Lily-of-the-Nile
30	Petunias
50	Sweet alyssum
24	Mealy cup sages

Regional plant alternatives on pages 119-123. For suggested fertilizers, see page 97.

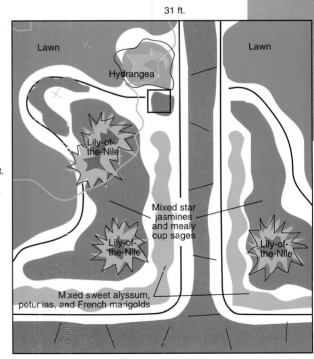

31 ft.

Lawn

Hydrangea

Lawn

35 ft.

Lily-of-the-Nile

Lily-of-the-Nile

Mixed star jasmines and mealy cup sages

Lily-of-the-Nile

Mixed sweet alyssum, petunias, and French marigolds

Q: The walkway that curves up to our house passes beneath tall maples. It's a cool, sheltered approach during the summer, but seems drab. How can we spruce up this area—the first thing our guests encounter—and make it more inviting?

A: Let your guests make a grand entrance through beds of shade-loving annuals. Their bright, cheerful colors and well-behaved forms will dress up even the plainest spot.

Prepare wide, curving beds with ample room for masses of flowers. Shade-loving plants need plenty of water and will droop quickly if left to dry out, so incorporate compost or other organic matter deep into the soil to help retain moisture. Too much standing water, however, also will stress plants; improve drainage, if necessary, by adding coarse sand. For greatest color impact, alternate broad bands of New Guinea impatiens, impatiens wallerana, and begonia, along with perennial ferns for contrast. Other colorful annual choices include coleus, primrose, and schizanthus, or perennials such as astilbe, azalea, or fuchsia. Once plants are in place, mulch heavily with pine needles or shredded bark to suppress weeds, keep roots cool, and cut down on watering chores.

WHAT YOU NEED:

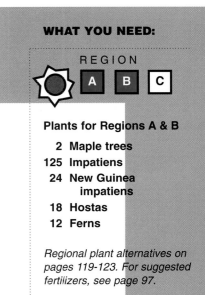

REGION

A   B   C

Plants for Regions A & B

2	Maple trees
125	Impatiens
24	New Guinea impatiens
18	Hostas
12	Ferns

Regional plant alternatives on pages 119-123. For suggested fertilizers, see page 97.

56 ft.

46 ft.

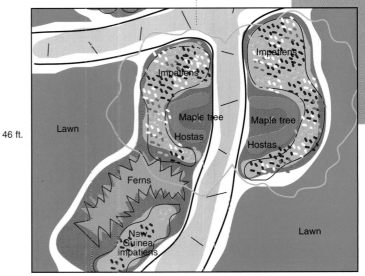

LOCATION
Side Yard

Q: The shaded area that runs along the side of our house is barren and neglected, though we use the area often to get to our back yard. How can we give it a more cultivated, serene appearance that will make it a pleasure to walk through?

A: Consider borrowing some quiet splendor from a Japanese garden where carefully placed rocks and plants lend a sense of timeless tranquility. Simplicity, repetition, and a limited color scheme also contribute to the meditative quality.

Begin by laying out a gently curving pathway, bordered with benderboard and filled with pebbles and stepping-stones. Cultivate the soil on each side of the walkway, and incorporate plenty of organic matter, including well-dampened peat moss. Border the walkway with clumps of ferns—include two types for a variety of leaf forms and hues—then stagger pink azaleas in between the ferns. If your soil is not acidic, work in Scotts® Azalea, Camellia, Rhododendron Planting Soil. For additional summer color, tuck in pink petunias at the bases of the ferns. To augment the Oriental atmosphere, include a Japanese maple and clumps of Japanese iris. Don't let these plants dry out; they all love rich, well-drained soil and ample water.

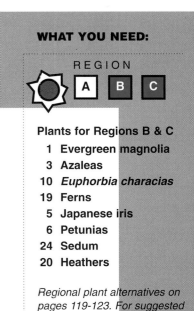

WHAT YOU NEED:

REGION

A B C

Plants for Regions B & C

1	Evergreen magnolia
3	Azaleas
10	*Euphorbia characias*
19	Ferns
5	Japanese iris
6	Petunias
24	Sedum
20	Heathers

Regional plant alternatives on pages 119-123. For suggested fertilizers, see page 97.

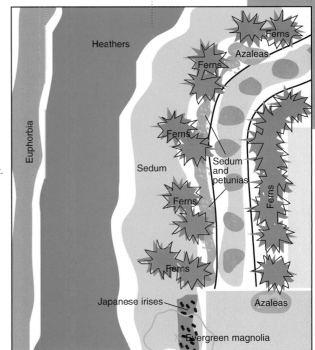

36 ft.

41 ft.

Heathers

Euphorbia

Ferns

Azaleas

Ferns

Ferns

Sedum

Sedum and petunias

Ferns

Ferns

Ferns

Japanese irises

Azaleas

Evergreen magnolia

Q: Because our house is on a corner lot, a large section of our side yard is open to the street. We'd like more privacy, as well as a pretty spot to relax on hot summer days, yet most side yards seem cramped and boring. Any suggestions?

A: Take possession of your side yard by enclosing it with a privacy fence. But instead of the expected straight fence along the property line, buck convention by setting sections of the fence at odd angles.

A zigzag fence can solve a multitude of site problems. You can skirt trees that stand in the way of a straight run, establish interesting corners for planting, bump out an area for a small patio, and create an illusion of space that isn't possible with a straight, narrow passageway. Gain additional visual space—and light—by painting your new fence white. While planning the layout of the yard inside the fence, include planting beds on each side of your walkway or patio. The fence and house are likely to cast long shadows, so mass together flowering shade plants, such as hosta, astilbe, and azalea, for best results. To provide an upward accent, include tall fountains of miscanthus, which will retain its sculptural beauty even in winter.

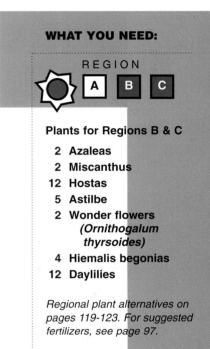

WHAT YOU NEED:

REGION
A B C

Plants for Regions B & C

  2 Azaleas
  2 Miscanthus
12 Hostas
  5 Astilbe
  2 Wonder flowers
    (Ornithogalum
      thyrsoides)
  4 Hiemalis begonias
12 Daylilies

Regional plant alternatives on pages 119-123. For suggested fertilizers, see page 97.

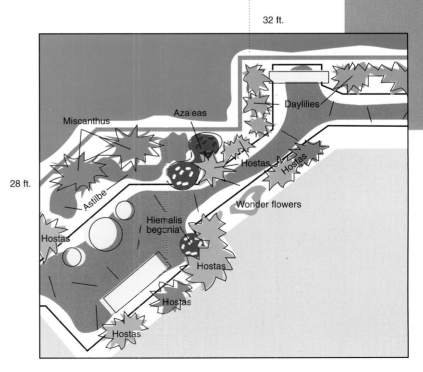

32 ft.

28 ft.

Miscanthus

Azaleas

Daylilies

Hostas

Hostas

Astilbe

Wonder flowers

Hiemalis begonia

Hostas

Hostas

Hostas

Hostas

LOCATION
Along the Foundation

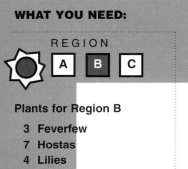

WHAT YOU NEED:

REGION

A **B** C

Plants for Region B

- 3 Feverfew
- 7 Hostas
- 4 Lilies
- 5 Astilbe
- 5 Solomon's seals
- 6 Ferns
- 1 Holly tree

Regional plant alternatives on pages 119-123. For suggested fertilizers, see page 97.

Regional plant alternatives on pages 119-123. For suggested fertilizers, see page 97.

Q: **We've had fun planning and planting most of our garden, but the bed along the north side of our house remains bare. What can we plant there along the foundation that will grow well in the shade of the house and nearby trees?**

A: Foundation plantings on the north side of a house can be a challenge, not only because of the shade but because of the climate. The soil in such spots often remains cold and damp well into spring, while flowers on the south side of the house are already flourishing. Luckily, some plants don't seem to mind the late start on the season.

Hostas are particularly well suited to foundation beds in north-facing locations. These rich, mounding plants are celebrated for their foliage, which varies from deep blue-green to golden yellow and can be ridged, smooth, matte, glossy, or variegated, depending on the variety. Hostas range in size from less than 6 inches to as much as 5 feet in height; plant taller specimens next to the house and use dwarf kinds along the outer edge of the bed. Equally well adapted is astilbe, as well as Solomon's seal, a slow-spreading perennial with arching stems and small, bell-shaped blossoms. All require regular summer watering. Watch that roof overhangs do not deny flowers rainfall.

15 ft.

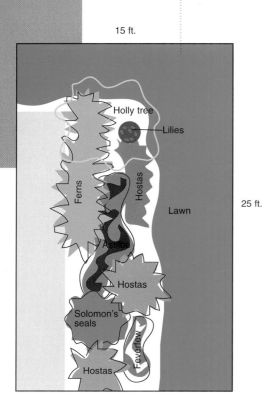

25 ft.

Q: Our lawn runs right up to the edge of our house, and the transition from grass to brick seems too abrupt. I'd prefer a softer look but don't want shrubs. I like lots of color during the summer, but it's the shaded north side of my house. What can I plant there?

A: For maximum color, choose annuals. You can enjoy their cheerful good looks all through the growing season.

Begin by preparing a 2- to 3-foot-wide planting bed, sloped slightly upward at the back. Incorporate compost or other organic matter to aid in retaining moisture, and add coarse sand if drainage is poor. Two of the top-performing annuals for shade are impatiens and coleus. Consider a one-color scheme, with an intense red color of impatiens combined with red variegated coleus. For fullest growth habit, pinch back both types of plants while young, and remove flower buds from coleus as soon as they appear. Keep soil moist and feed plants regularly. If you have window boxes, take special care to check soil moisture every day. Window boxes dry out very easily.

WHAT YOU NEED:

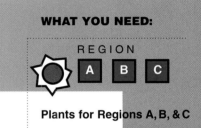

REGION
A B C

Plants for Regions A, B, & C

46 Impatiens
 3 Hostas
 6 Begonias
 9 Coleus
12 Ground ivies

Regional plant alternatives on pages 119-123. For suggested fertilizers, see page 97.

24 ft.

13 ft.

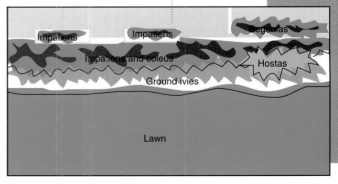

WHAT YOU NEED:

REGION

A B C

Plants for Regions B & C

1 **Dogwood**
7 **Azaleas**
5 **Gooseneck loosestrife**
3 **Miniature roses**
1 **Yucca**
3 **Cotoneasters**
1 **Japanese maple**
1 **Houttuynia**
10 *Verbena peruviana*
3 **Artemisia**

Regional plant alternatives on pages 119-123. For suggested fertilizers, see page 97.

Q: The very lightly shaded pathway that leads to the rear of our property gets a lot of traffic, but has only a few small trees alongside it to lend visual interest. How can we make it a more pleasant place to walk?

A: To add to your path's eye appeal, add a broad edging of easy-care perennials, chosen for their mounding forms or low-spreading habit. Plants such as *Verbena peruviana*, cotoneaster, daylily, and the miniature rose will thrive in your sunniest spots, while azalea, variegated houttuynia, and gooseneck loosestrife will make themselves at home in sections that receive part shade. If necessary, add organic material to the soil; azaleas, in particular, will feel more at home if you work in peat moss before planting them.

When setting out all plants, pay careful attention to their eventual spread at maturity; locate specimens like creeping cotoneaster well back from the walkway to avoid having to prune them at the pathway's edge. Plants with spiky foliage, such as variegated yucca, also should be situated with care so you don't get pricked as you pass by. Gooseneck loosestrife will eventually spread; plant it where it won't overwhelm its neighbors.

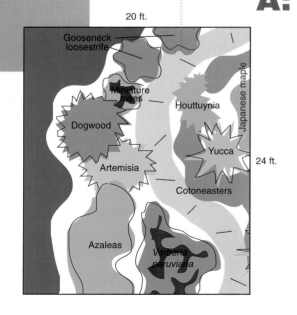

20 ft.

Gooseneck loosestrife

Miniature roses

Houttuynia

Japanese maple

Dogwood

Yucca

24 ft.

Artemisia

Cotoneasters

Azaleas

Verbena peruviana

Q: The plain brick pathway that leads to a shaded seating area at the back of our property has little charm or romance. I want it to be more lush and inviting—almost tropical in feeling. Can I do that with readily available plants?

A: The lure of the jungle can indeed be re-created along the edges of your shady path with plants you can find at almost any nursery that handles perennials. Lush foliage is what you should look for, along with flowers that have an exotic, tropical appearance.

Ferns, in particular, evoke the feeling of the jungle or forest floor. Though tropical in character, many will weather winter in style, provided you choose varieties suited to your area. Ostrich ferns, for instance, put on their best show in areas where winters are cold. The bright, fluffy plumes of astilbe also have exotic appeal and will thrive in your moist, shaded site. For height at the back of your walkway border, choose yellow rocket ligularia. Try additional plants if your winters are mild; Japanese aralia, acanthus, or *Rhodea japonica* all have showy, tropical-looking foliage.

WHAT YOU NEED:

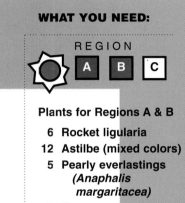

REGION
A B C

Plants for Regions A & B

6 Rocket ligularia
12 Astilbe (mixed colors)
5 Pearly everlastings
    **(Anaphalis
    margaritacea)**
2 Ferns

Regional plant alternatives on pages 119-123. For suggested fertilizers, see page 97.

We'll be hosting our daughter's wedding in a few months, and the reception will be in our garden. All is looking fine except for a shady bed under our oak tree. What can I plant there that will give me lots of color—fast?

A: Annuals are tops when it comes to quick results, even for the shade. For the utmost in performance, however, they need well-prepared soil, rich in humus. If the soil in your bed is sandy or heavy with clay, incorporate additional organic matter before setting out plants.

For masses of bright flowers, choose impatiens to fill most of your shady bed. The single-flowering type, in particular, explodes with blooms in pale pink, fuchsia, rose, white, orange, or lavender. For quickest color, choose nursery plants in 4-inch pots; small plants from pony packs will take longer to perform. Edge the bed with clumping or trailing lobelia. These popular plants have tiny flowers in shades from the palest blue to intense sapphire that contrast well with the pink hues of impatiens. Other fast-bloomers that thrive in the shade include monkey flower *(Mimulus hybridus)*, schizanthus, primrose, and cineraria. All of these prefer ample moisture.

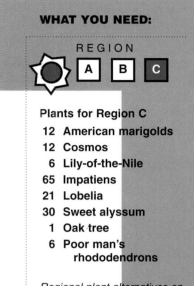

WHAT YOU NEED:

REGION

A B C

Plants for Region C

12	American marigolds
12	Cosmos
6	Lily-of-the-Nile
65	Impatiens
21	Lobelia
30	Sweet alyssum
1	Oak tree
6	Poor man's rhododendrons

Regional plant alternatives on pages 119-123. For suggested fertilizers, see page 97.

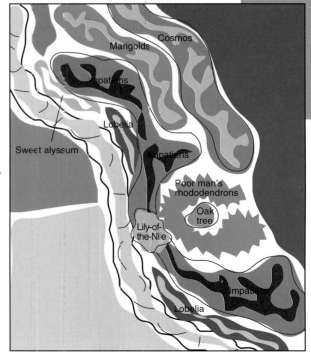

32 ft.

39 ft.

Q: **We have a yard with lots of fully grown trees and shrubs, yet I'd love to have more flowers along the pathway that leads through the shadiest part of our lot. What can I plant that won't require a lot of work?**

A: One of the fastest ways to bring bright color to a shaded spot is with a bed of flowering annuals suited to low-light conditions. They must be replanted each year, but their dazzling color is worth the extra effort. Keep beds small—just a foot-wide border is enough to make great impact—and you'll reduce planting chores to a minimum.

Shade-loving annuals prefer rich, well-drained soil, so prepare planting beds well, then add additional organic matter each time the beds are cultivated. A few annuals are favorites for shaded areas; most frequently chosen for its brilliant hues and masses of flowers is impatiens. Double-flowering types are available, but single-flowering types will produce the most blossoms. Other spectacular choices for shady conditions include primula, cineraria, schizanthus, and monkey flower *(Mimulus hybridus)*. Many of these annuals boast flowers in a variety of colors, so a mix of plant types is unnecessary.

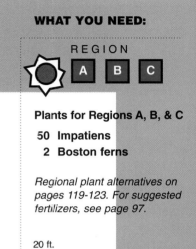

WHAT YOU NEED:

REGION A B C

Plants for Regions A, B, & C

50 Impatiens
2 Boston ferns

Regional plant alternatives on pages 119-123. For suggested fertilizers, see page 97.

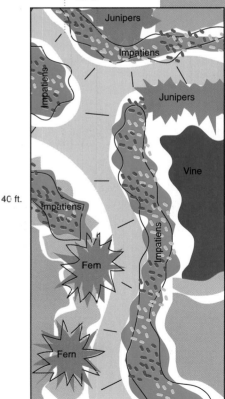

Q: The pathway that leads around the shaded side of my house doesn't get a lot of traffic. But when I do take friends around that way, I'd like to have it look nurtured, not neglected. What can I plant that won't need a lot of maintenance?

A: For the fewest maintenance chores, think in terms of plants that will cover the ground entirely, shading out weeds and keeping in moisture. But don't settle for functionality alone; your choices also should provide color in the form of flowers or variegated foliage.

Lush, leafy hostas perform beautifully on all three counts; available varieties range from less than 6 inches in height to more than 5 feet tall. (Bait well for snails and slugs, which adore these plants.) Other top shade-performers include astilbe, with its airy plumes of pink, peach, lavender, red, or white flowers, and the groundcover leadwort, which puts forth bright blue flowers from late summer to first frost. An added plus: The leaves of this spreading groundcover turn an attractive deep red in the fall. For permanent plantings, good soil preparation is essential; all of these plants require plenty of organic matter in the soil and ample summer water.

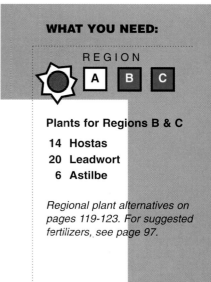

WHAT YOU NEED:

REGION

A   B   C

Plants for Regions B & C

14 Hostas
20 Leadwort
6 Astilbe

Regional plant alternatives on pages 119-123. For suggested fertilizers, see page 97.

23 ft.

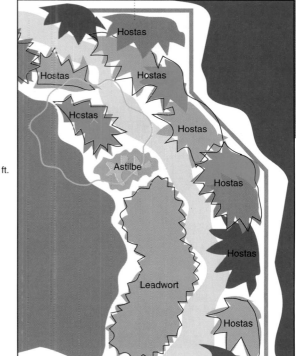

30 ft.

Q: The rear section of our lot is heavily wooded and is shaded during most of the day. We love the trees (it's so cool there during the worst of summer) but have a hard time getting other plants to grow there. Can you help?

A: When faced with a tough landscaping problem, sometimes it's best to follow nature's lead. Rather than fighting the trees, rely instead on woodland plants that grow wild in such cool, shaded conditions. Most likely, the soil in your wooded spot already is rich in organic material (the benefit of years of fallen leaves). but amend it with additional peat moss or compost if the ground is compacted or sandy. Woodland plants won't flourish unless their roots are pampered with ample nutrients and moisture.

Choose plants, such as royal fern, to provide lush greenery, but also be sure to include flowering woodland beauties, such as bleeding heart, columbine, Virginia bluebell, violet, and trillium. Mulch around plants heavily with pine needles or shredded bark to conserve moisture and keep roots cool. Then, so you can enjoy this quiet sanctuary, set out a meandering pathway of redwood rounds and tuck in a rustic bench for relaxing on those hot summer days.

WHAT YOU NEED:

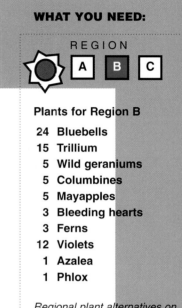

REGION

A **B** C

Plants for Region B

24 **Bluebells**
15 **Trillium**
 5 **Wild geraniums**
 5 **Columbines**
 5 **Mayapples**
 3 **Bleeding hearts**
 3 **Ferns**
12 **Violets**
 1 **Azalea**
 1 **Phlox**

Regional plant alternatives on pages 119-123. For suggested fertilizers, see page 97.

30 ft.

35 ft.

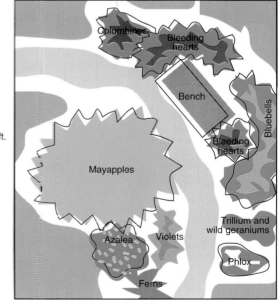

Q: Our tiny house seems a perfect candidate for an old-fashioned cottage garden overflowing with exuberant masses of flowers. But, except for a few sunny spots, we mostly have light shade. Will traditional flowers survive here?

A: The traditional cottage gardens of England often are filled with shade-tolerant plants, accustomed to thriving under cloudy skies. Many favorites, such as foxglove, even will naturalize under such low-light conditions.

Observe your garden spot with care, noting which areas are shadiest and which receive the most sun. Then locate sun-loving cottage-garden plants, such as delphiniums and roses, where they'll enjoy at least a half-day of direct light. Reserve the rest of the garden for more flexible old-fashioned bloomers, such as wallflower, gas plant, lychnis, campanula, daylily, or nicotiana. Other good choices for filtered light include astilbe, meadow rue, Johnny-jump-up, and forget-me-not. Don't be afraid to mix plants of different heights and forms; cottage gardens get much of their charm from their haphazard look. Drifts of color, however, work better than isolated spots of color; for best effect, mass plants such as foxglove or delphinium together.

WHAT YOU NEED:

REGION
A **B** C

Plants for Region B

- 1 Dogwood tree
- 2 Climbing roses
- 6 Bush roses
- 10 Gas plants
- 6 Delphiniums
- 8 Wallflowers
- 3 Foxglove
- 2 Ferns

Regional plant alternatives on pages 119-123. For suggested fertilizers, see page 97.

24 ft.

23 ft.

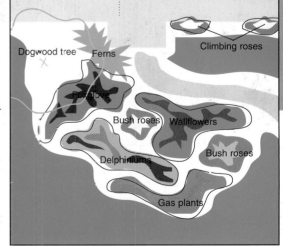

**STYLE
OF GARDEN**
Informal

Q: The towering maple trees in our back yard provide wonderful protection from summer's heat, but most of what we plant beneath them gets leggy and weak. How can we create a lush but informal garden where plants will thrive?

A: Many gardeners try to fight the shade and end up with spindly plants that stretch to reach the sun. Instead, give in to the cool pleasures of your site. Shade-loving plants will reward you with jewel-like greenery and delicate blooms of intense hues, provided you give them rich, well-drained soil and ample summer water.

If you're going for the informal look, rather than planning too carefully by laying out formal beds of hostas and astilbe beneath your trees, fill broad expanses of the garden with loose mounds of color. Mix lush fronds of ferns with spires of campanula or foxglove, and border meandering pathways with lady's-mantle or bloody cranes-bill geraniums. For height, tuck rhododendrons back among the trees, and front them with daylilies or Shasta daisies—sun-loving plants that also perform in filtered shade. Patches of moss will enhance the woodland feeling, and architectural ornaments—tall columns, tumbled stone walls, or statuary—will create the aura of an ancient, forgotten garden spot.

WHAT YOU NEED:

REGION
A B C

Plants for Regions A & B

- 3 Dwarf redleaf Japanese barberries
- 2 Red shrub roses
- 4 Campanula
- 3 Ferns
- 2 Lady's-mantles
- 6 *Geranium sanguineum*
- 4 Shasta daisies
- 6 Pinks
- 3 Camomile
- 2 Daylilies
- 2 Feverfews

Regional plant alternatives on pages 119-123. For suggested fertilizers, see page 97.

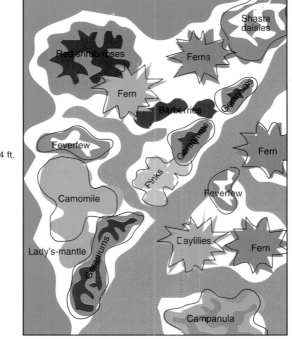

26 ft.

34 ft.

Shasta daisies · Red shrub roses · Ferns · Fern · Geraniums · Barberries · Geraniums · Feverfew · Fern · Pinks · Feverfew · Camomile · Daylilies · Fern · Geraniums · Lady's-mantle · Campanula

Q: Our lawn thins out where it meets the shade of our pine trees, leaving a scraggly edge. We'd like to give that section of our yard a more polished look. But if grass struggles to survive there, do we dare plant anything else?

A: Your grass may not thrive in the filtered shade of the pines, but there are many rewarding plants that will. If you concentrate on filling this transitional zone with shade-loving perennials, you'll reap their tidy benefits for years to come.

Trim the edge of the lawn into a pleasing curve where the grass begins to thin, then augment a broad band of soil in front of the trees with peat moss, compost, or other organic matter. Add coarse sand to promote drainage; most shade-loving plants like moist conditions but hate having soggy feet. Choose plants from among dozens of varieties of hosta, astilbe, and fern; mass plants together for impact and keep in mind that leaf texture, color, and shape all can add visual interest. Plants such as variegated euonymus will do best at the front of the border, where the light is brightest, just as tall rhododendrons are likely to flourish back among the trees.

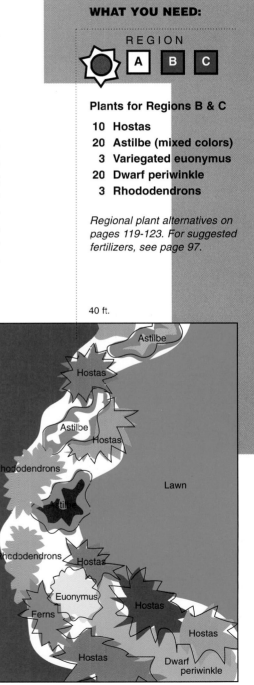

WHAT YOU NEED:

REGION

A   B   C

Plants for Regions B & C

10	Hostas
20	Astilbe (mixed colors)
3	Variegated euonymus
20	Dwarf periwinkle
3	Rhododendrons

Regional plant alternatives on pages 119-123. For suggested fertilizers, see page 97.

40 ft.

58 ft.

Astilbe
Hostas
Astilbe
Hostas
Rhododendrons
Astilbe
Lawn
Rhododendrons
Hostas
Euonymus
Hostas
Ferns
Hostas
Hostas
Dwarf periwinkle

Q: My somewhat shaded yard certainly doesn't qualify as a desert, but the spot is parched for much of the year. How can I grow some pretty, traditional flowers without spending all my time on watering chores?

A: Concentrate plants in small areas of your yard for maximum impact with a minimum of watering. Begin by replacing grass or large areas of groundcover with broad flagstone walkways or a brick or stone patio, leaving only corners of the yard—or small borders—free for planting. Amend the soil in those spots as needed; your goal is a soil that drains quickly and doesn't become soggy, but has plenty of organic matter to hold moisture where plants can use it.

For bright masses of color, you might want to experiment with traditional annuals that tolerate filtered shade; you can avoid transplanting chores by sowing seeds of such plants as larkspur or annual delphinium, dwarf nasturtium, zinnia, and dusty miller in place. (Check seed packages for recommended planting times in your area.) Accent with tall, bold bloomers, such as lilies; add extra organic matter before planting bulbs, and keep the soil moist throughout the year. Lilies prefer cool roots, so be sure to plant them where they'll be shaded by other established plants.

WHAT YOU NEED:

REGION

A B C

Plants for Regions A & B

25 **Larkspur**
6 **Petunias**
6 **Lobelia**
7 **Dusty millers**
8 **Zinnias**
2 **Lilies**
15 **Nasturtiums**

Regional plant alternatives on pages 119-123. For suggested fertilizers, see page 97.

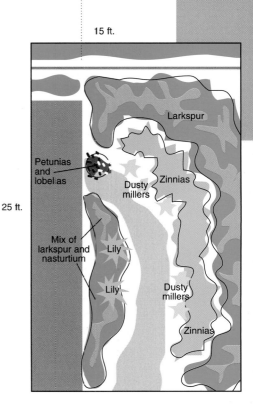

15 ft.

25 ft.

Larkspur

Petunias and lobelias

Zinnias

Dusty millers

Mix of larkspur and nasturtium

Lily

Lily

Dusty millers

Zinnias

Q: Compared with the rest of our yard, the hillside that slopes away from our lawn looks barren and unkempt. The spot is in shade much of the day, but the soil is rather dry. How can we give this neglected area a more cultivated look?

A: Sloping sites are tailor-made for rock gardens planted with a variety of spiked and ground-hugging plants. Most rock gardens, however, are situated in full sunshine, so your lightly shaded spot will take a bit more care when it comes time to choose appropriate plants.

Begin by buying a trio or quintet of large rocks (look under Rocks or Landscaping Supplies in the phone book), and have them professionally moved and placed on your site. Though sizable specimens are expensive, their permanent impact on the landscape justifies their price. Surround the rocks with shade-tolerant plants that aren't too picky about water; your sloping site ensures fast drainage. Choices include showy plants such as sedum, daylily, or cranesbill; groundcovers such as vinca, ajuga, or barren strawberry; and bushes such as flowering currant or viburnum. If the fringes of your slope are sunny, include spiky liatris or low-growing junipers. Mulch to prevent erosion.

49 **SPECIAL CONDITIONS**
Slope

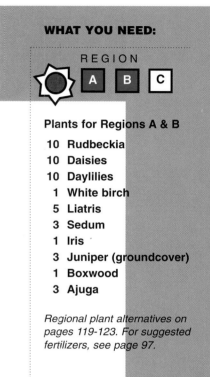

WHAT YOU NEED:

REGION

A B C

Plants for Regions A & B

10 **Rudbeckia**
10 **Daisies**
10 **Daylilies**
 1 **White birch**
 5 **Liatris**
 3 **Sedum**
 1 **Iris**
 3 **Juniper (groundcover)**
 1 **Boxwood**
 3 **Ajuga**

Regional plant alternatives on pages 119-123. For suggested fertilizers, see page 97.

35 ft.

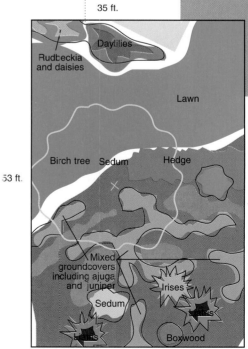

53 ft.

Q: Though it's surrounded by beautiful shade trees, our large back yard seems too open and empty. I'd love to fill it with flowers and make it feel more intimate, but I'm unsure what to plant, and where. Any ideas?

A: Begin by outlining wide, curving beds along the perimeter of the yard, leaving your existing lawn in the middle. Later, after outer beds are established, diminish your sprawling space by adding an island bed in the middle of the yard. Wide, grassy pathways between inner and outer beds (left over from your lawn) will make exploring the garden's nooks and crannies a pleasure, and the island bed will fill the heart of your yard with color from spring through fall.

Prepare soil by digging in plenty of organic matter to help retain moisture. Then choose from among tried-and-true shade-lovers such as astilbe and hosta; many varieties of each are available. Don't overlook the effects of foliage. Hostas, in particular, come in many shades of green and often boast striking, variegated leaves. Mulch heavily around plants to keep roots cool. For a lush, overgrown look and a heightened sense of privacy, tuck some rhododendrons among the trees along the fence line of your property.

WHAT YOU NEED:

REGION

A   B   C

Plants for Regions A, B, & C

20	Hostas
18	Astilbe (mixed colors)
15	Daylilies
2	Rhododendrons
1	Mugo pine
12	Campanula
1	Juniper
1	Bleeding heart
1	Azalea

Regional plant alternatives on pages 119-123. For suggested fertilizers, see page 97.

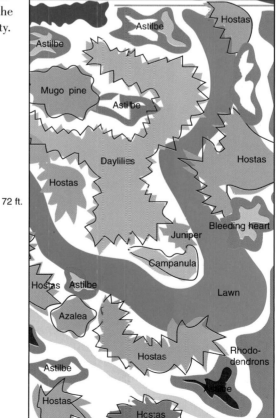

40 ft.

72 ft.

Flower Basics

W HETHER YOU'RE NEW TO FLOWER GARDENING OR YOUR GREEN THUMB IS FADING, RELY on this chapter for helpful advice. We begin with a discussion of soil composition and fertility. Following that is planting and maintenance information for all of the different flower types.

ANALYZING YOUR SOIL

Good soil is as important to your lawn and garden as a good foundation is to your house. Before you begin, you should know something about the composition of your soil.

Soil is composed of four primary ingredients: sand, clay, silt, and organic matter or humus. Your soil type is determined by its proportions of these four materials. If you have too much clay in your soil, it will not till or drain well. If you have too much sand in your soil, it won't retain enough moisture for your plants to grow. If you pick up a handful of your soil and you can squeeze it into a tight, sticky mass, it is high in clay. A loose, crumbly soil that won't hold any shape has a high sand content. Ideal soil is a dark and light mixture of sand, clay, and a generous helping of organic material.

The best way to improve your soil's physical characteristics is to work in organic matter (or humus), such as Scotts® 3-in-1 Organic Mix. If you add organic matter to sandy soil, it will improve water retention. If you add it to clay soil, it improves drainage and workability. However, because none of these organic materials contains many plant nutrients, you shouldn't use them in place of fertilizer.

Loam (top), the ideal soil, molds into a loose mound when squeezed lightly. Squeezed harder, however, it crumbles. Sandy soil (center) feels grainy and crumbles when wet. Soil high in clay (bottom) forms a tight, sticky mass if squeezed when wet.

FERTILIZING YOUR GARDEN

Soil fertility is just as important to your garden as soil composition. Consider these products when improving your soil:

Scotts Granular Plant Foods: Scotts granular plant foods are slow-release fertilizers thatcan be mixed in with the soil when planting, or simply spread around established plants.

Scotts Ready-to-Use Liquids: Scotts ready-to-use liquid is a snap to use. Simply connect it to your hose and spray. Promote vigorous plants and beautiful blooms with these handy fertilizers.

Peters® Professional® Plant Foods: Peters water-soluble plant foods are the same products three out of four professional growers prefer to use. Peters plant foods are fully soluble so no clogging occurs in your feeder. Peters rich feeding of nitrogen, phosphorus, potassium, and micronutrients produces full, lush plants that will be the envy of your neighbors.

Once® Season-Long Plant Foods: Once Season-Long plant foods are granular fertilizers that produce a slow-release feeding of primary nutrients and minor nutrients for an entire plant season. Just apply this fertilizer once and get beautiful blooms and lush foliage for the entire season.

Osmocote® Plant Foods: Osmocote plant foods provide the ultimate in extended-release fertilizers. These products provide your plants a balanced diet for up to a full year. This convenient line allows you to feed your plants once a season without the danger of over- or underfeeding.

Note: Groundcovers fall into many different plant categories. Feed groundcovers according to the plant group to which they belong—for example, perennials or woody plants.

FERTILIZER CHART

Plant Group	Feeding Schedule*	Scotts Granular Plant Foods	Scotts Ready-to-Use Liquids	Peters Professional Water Solubles	Once Season-Long Plant Foods	Osmocote Plant Foods
Annuals	*Spring and Summer*	Flower Food	Rose & Flowering Shrub Plant Food	All-Purpose Plant Food or Super Blossom Booster	Vegetables & Bedding Plants	Vegetable & Bedding Plant Food
Berries	*Prior to Spring Growth*	Fruit and Berry Food	All-Purpose Plant Food	All-Purpose Plant Food	Vegetables & Bedding Plants	Outdoor & Indoor Plant Food
Bulbs, Tubers	*Planting Time and After Flowering*	Bulb Food	All-Purpose Plant Food	All-Purpose Plant Food	Roses & Flowering Plants	Vegetable & Bedding Plant Food
Evergreens	*Late Spring and Fall*	Evergreen Shrub & Tree Food	Azalea, Evergreen, Rhododendron, Holly Plant Food	All-Purpose Plant Food	Trees, Shrubs & Evergreens	Tree & Shrub Planting Tablets
Perennials	*Early Spring and Mid-Summer*	Flower Food	Rose & Flowering Shrub Plant Food	All-Purpose Plant Food or Super Blossom Booster	Roses & Flowering Plants	Outdoor & Indoor Plant Food
Trees	*Late Spring and Fall*	Evergreen Shrub & Tree Food	All-Purpose Plant Food	All-Purpose Plant Food	Trees, Shrubs & Evergreens	Tree & Shrub Planting Tablets
Palms	*Spring, Summer and Fall*	Palm Food				
Woody Plants (such as Shrubs and Trees)	*Early Spring*	All-Purpose Plant Food	Azalea, Evergreen, Rhododendron, Holly Plant Food	All-Purpose Plant Food	Trees, Shrubs & Evergreens	Tree & Shrub Planting Tablets
Azaleas, Camellias, Rhododendrons	*Early Spring and Summer*	Azalea, Camellia, Rhododendron Food	Azalea, Evergreen, Rhododendron, Holly Plant Food	Azalea, Camellia & Rhododendron Food	Roses & Flowering Plants	Outdoor & Indoor Plant Food
Roses	*Early Spring, Late Spring and Mid-Summer*	Rose Food	Rose & Flowering Shrub Plant Food	Rose Food	Roses & Flowering Plants	Outdoor & Indoor Plant Food

* Always read fertilizer instructions prior to feeding.

ANNUALS AND PERENNIALS

Most flowers are broadly designated as either annuals or perennials. Annuals complete their life cycle in one season—they sprout, grow, bloom, and die. The above-ground foliage of perennials dies off at the end of each season, but the roots send up new foliage—and new blooms—year after year. Here's how to plant and maintain the plants featured in the plans on pages 6-95.

PLANTING ANNUALS

PREPARING THE SOIL

Annuals don't require the intensive soil preparation that perennials do, but the better the soil, the better they'll grow and bloom. Good soil contains lots of organic material, providing plants with the loose, rich environment they need to thrive. Clay and sand are much improved by digging in organic amendments, such as compost, shredded leaves, manure, peat moss, ground bark, or a combination of these. Look for Scotts® planting soils, which contain excellent mixtures of many of these organic amendments. Cover the soil with a 2- to 4-inch layer of organic material and work it in to a depth of

6 to 12 inches with a shovel, spade, turning fork, or rotary tiller. In light soils, such as sand, a garden spade works well; in heavy soils, such as clay, a turning fork is easier to use. For large areas, a rotary tiller helps prevent a creaky back the next morning. Once the soil is turned, rake it smooth, crushing clods and removing rocks.

CHOOSING HEALTHY NURSERY PLANTS

Annuals in most nurseries and garden centers come in a variety of sizes: small, molded-plastic six-packs called pony packs, a larger version called a jumbo,

4-inch pots called fours, and gallon-size containers. Ordinarily, the smaller the plant, the lower the price. Since annuals tend to be fast-growing, the pony packs and jumbo sizes are often a good buy simply because they don't take long to catch up with the gallon-size plants and because they cost much less. Look for bushy, well-budded plants. While the temptation is always to pick the tallest plants with the most flowers, these plants don't transplant as well or bloom as long in the garden. Skip any plants that have yellowing or dead leaves, signs of disease; tall stems with no leaves (the proper term for such plants is "leggy"), or that show signs of stress, such as wilting or sun-scalded leaves.

Nursery-grown plants should be planted as soon as possible after purchase. A long spell in the car does not improve them nor does a stint on a patio or deck for several weeks. See suggestions for planting under "Transplanting Seedlings" on the next page.

Left: Though it's tempting to buy plants with the biggest blooms, purchase plants with sturdy foliage instead. They'll bloom better in the long run.

Below: Annuals provide bright color late into the growing season.

Top: If planting from flats, use a sharp knife to cut the roots apart or tease the roots out carefully with a kitchen fork.

Bottom: When planting seeds, follow the instructions on the seed packet explicitly. Some seeds need to be covered, but others must be sown on the surface because they need light to germinate.

STARTING SEEDS

Start seeds indoors using damp planter mix, such as Scotts® Seed Starter Potting Soil, and clean pony packs or foam egg cartons. Follow the instructions on the seed packet explicitly; some seeds need to be covered, but others must be planted on the soil surface because they need light to germinate. Place containers in a bright, cool place, such as a windowsill, and keep the soil moist, but not wet, once the seeds sprout. It may be best to use a mister at first to avoid washing the seeds out of the soil.

Some seeds can be broadcast or planted where they will grow in the garden; the seed packet will state whether the seeds should be started indoors or outdoors in your climate zone. Save the seed packet. On the back is information on how far apart to space the seedlings when they are transplanted outside.

Another option is Scotts PatchMaster® Garden Seeding Mixes. These products include seed, mulch, and fertilizer in one ready-to-use combination. Simply spread and water for beautiful patches of flowers.

TRANSPLANTING SEEDLINGS

Once the seedlings have produced their second set of leaves and all danger of frost is past, harden them off by putting them outside in a sheltered, shady spot for a week. This helps acclimate the seedlings to outside conditions.

Prepare the planting bed before transplanting the seedlings into the garden. Transplant a day or two after rain, on a cloudy day, or late in the afternoon—hot midday sun can scald or wilt new transplants.

Immediately before planting, soak the plants thoroughly. Dig holes slightly bigger than the root ball, and puddle each hole (fill it with water and let it drain). Slip each seedling out of the pot, one at a time, and tuck it straight into its hole. Tap or press the bottom of the pot to slide the root ball out intact; pulling on the stem may tear the plant apart. Put the roots in the hole level with the soil and firm the moist soil around them carefully, making sure there are no air pockets.

Most seedlings do best set at the same level they were growing in the pot, although some do better when set with the stem below the level of the soil—right up to their bottom leaves. The buried stem sends out new roots, making for a sturdier, better-anchored plant. Check your seed package for which method to use.

If planting from flats, use a sharp knife to cut the roots apart or tease the roots out carefully with a kitchen fork.

Leave enough space between plants for each to grow to full size. After planting, water the transplants gently and thoroughly. (Get seedlings off to a good start with Scotts Transplant Food.) If birds are likely to pose a problem, use bird netting over the seedlings, and weight the edges with rocks or bricks.

CHOOSING SEEDLINGS

Plant only the strongest seedlings—those with straight, sturdy stems and healthy leaves. Discard any that are weak, broken, or damaged. See "Choosing Healthy Nursery Plants" on page 98 for what to look for.

THINNING SEEDLINGS

Seeds sown directly into the garden often need thinning in order to leave enough room for each plant to grow to its mature size. If there are more seedlings than needed to fill the space allotted, simply snip the extras out with a pair of small scissors. If there is space to plant the surplus seedlings, pry them out gently with a Popsicle stick, poke a new hole, and replant immediately. Handle seedlings by the leaves to avoid crushing the stem. Keep the soil moist—but not wet—until the seedlings are well established.

MAINTAINING ANNUALS

MULCHING

The purpose of mulch is to keep the soil cool and moist and reduce the number of weeds. The best mulches are made of composted material or ground-bark products. You can dig organic mulches such as these into the soil each year to improve it.

WATERING ANNUALS

The easiest way to water annuals is to install a drip-irrigation system and put it on a timer. In small areas, hand-watering with a hose and nozzle set on a gentle spray may be most efficient. Water larger areas with a fan or rotary sprinkler attached to a hose. In any case, always water until the soil is well soaked and let it dry out between waterings.

PINCHING

Pinching or pinching back is the process of nipping out the smallest pair of leaves on each branch. It causes the plant to put out new growth, making it fuller and bushier. Because many plants flower on new growth, it also can encourage more flowers. Sometimes pinching is used to direct growth.

Deadheading encourages a longer period of bloom by preventing the plant from setting seed.

DEADHEADING

Deadheading is the process of removing old blooms; its purpose is to encourage a longer period of bloom by preventing the plant from setting seed. Annuals can be deadheaded by nipping off the old flower simply by using your thumbnail and forefinger. To remove both flower and stem, a pair of scissors is useful.

STAKING ANNUALS

Some annuals require staking to keep them from flopping onto the ground. Delphiniums, foxglove, and tall dahlias are all candidates for staking. Tall, sturdy wooden stakes are best put in at the time of planting; this avoids damaging the roots when the flowers are tall enough to need the stakes. Tie the plants with green horticultural string or plastic plant ties—loosely enough to allow for growth, but tightly enough to keep them upright.

Smaller plants can be staked with wire stakes that have an open loop at the top to hold the stem. Because these stakes are so slender, you can insert them when they're needed without damaging roots. (Do be careful not to pierce the bulbs of spring tulips or summer lilies, however.)

FEEDING

Annuals don't need much feeding, but a balanced fertilizer can help plants put on sturdy growth and set more buds. All fertilizers list the three major ingredients in the same order: nitrogen, phosphorus, and potassium (potash). Nitrogen encourages growth of leaves and stems, while phosphorus and potassium increase flowering and root growth. Fertilizers are labeled according to the percentages of each of the ingredients they contain. See the chart on page 97 for a listing of the best kinds of plant foods for a given plant. Most annuals can make it through the growing season with one or two feedings.

Top: To transplant perennials from plastic pots, dig a hole that's twice as wide as the root ball.

Center: Slip the root ball into the hole, fill in any spaces with loose soil, and tamp it firmly around the roots.

Bottom: Water, allow the soil to settle, and add more soil, if necessary. Water again after applying Scotts Transplant Food.

WEEDING

To enjoy the full beauty of annual flowers, keep the beds cleared of weeds. Weeds are easiest to pull when they are small and when the ground is thoroughly wet. Mulches help keep weeds from coming up in the first place. To keep weeding from turning into a dreaded chore, pull a few weeds every time you're in the garden. It prevents weeds from running rampant and getting out of hand.

PLANTING PERENNIALS

PREPARING THE SOIL

Perennials are permanent residents in the garden, so it's worthwhile to prepare the soil well. Good soil contains lots of organic material, providing plants with the loose, rich soil they need to thrive. Clay and sand are much improved by digging in organic amendments, such as compost, shredded leaves, manure, peat moss, ground bark, or a combination of these. Any of the Scotts planting soils are perfect for adding rich mixtures of organic material to your soil.

Cover the soil with a 4- to 6-inch layer of organic material, and work it in to a depth of 12 to 18 inches with a shovel, spade, turning fork, or rotary tiller. In light soils, such as sand, a garden spade works well; in heavy soils, such as clay, a turning fork is easier to use. For large areas, a rotary tiller can do the job both easier and faster.

Once the soil is turned, rake it smooth, crushing clods and removing rocks. If you find that the soil is difficult to amend—for example, heavy clay on a slope—you may find it easier to build a raised bed and fill it with a good topsoil. Look for Scotts 3-in-1 Organic Mix, which is a substitute for topsoil mixtures.

CHOOSING HEALTHY NURSERY PLANTS

Most nurseries and garden centers carry perennials in 4-inch pots and in 1-gallon, 2-gallon, and 5-gallon plastic containers. Large shrubs may be purchased in 15-gallon plastic containers. Ordinarily, the smaller the pot, the lower the price. In general, smaller perennials tolerate transplanting better than larger ones, but larger plants provide immediate impact in the garden. Look for bushy, well-shaped plants that are in proportion to the pot; large plants in small pots may be root-bound, a condition characterized by masses of circling roots in the pot. While the temptation is always to pick the biggest plants with the most flowers, these plants don't transplant as well or bloom as long in the garden. Pass up perennials that have yellowing or dead leaves, signs of disease, tall stems with no leaves (the proper term for such plants is "leggy"), or that show signs of stress, such as wilting or sun-scalded leaves.

Nursery-grown plants should be planted as soon as possible after purchase. Pots dry out quickly if they are not watered conscientiously, and a day or two of forgetfulness can cost you the plant.

TRANSPLANTING PERENNIALS

Sometimes perennials are sold in six-packs; transplant these according to the directions given under "Transplanting Seedlings" on page 99. Plants in larger containers should be watered thoroughly before transplanting. It's best to have the hole dug before removing the plant from its pot. Dig a hole slightly

larger than the root ball, fill it with water, and allow it to drain. If the plants are in metal cans, have the cans cut at the nursery, and plant them as soon as you get home; it's next to impossible to keep cut cans adequately watered. Tap plants in plastic pots firmly on the bottom, and slide the root ball out of the pot carefully. Slip the root ball into the hole. Fill in any spaces with loose soil, and tamp it firmly around the roots. Water, allow the soil to settle, and add more soil, if necessary. Water again after applying fertilizer. Be sure to plant the perennial at the same level it was growing in the pot; covering the crown (the point where the stem and roots meet) can kill some plants.

MAINTAINING PERENNIALS

MULCHING

Mulch perennials with organic materials such as compost and ground-bark products. Organic mulches will break down in the soil, enriching it and improving drainage. Mulching perennials serves several purposes: It keeps soil temperatures more even in cold-winter climates; it keeps weeds to

One of the best things about perennials—plants whose foliage dies off every year, but whose roots send up new foliage and blooms every spring—is their easy care. Once they're planted, all you need to do to keep them in top-notch condition is to fertilize them regularly and divide them once every few years.

AZALEAS, CAMELLIAS, AND RHODODENDRONS

All grow best in partial shade.

If they get direct sun, make sure it is only early-morning sun, and then for no longer than a few hours. They do well under tall trees or on the north side of the house.

All grow best in acid soil.

That is soil with a pH of 6.0 or lower. Soil-testing kits are available from many garden centers or your local extension agent (often listed in the telephone book under County Services). Increase soil acidity by digging pine needles into the soil or laying down a pine-needle mulch.

All benefit from regular feeding.

Apply Scotts® Azalea, Camellia, Rhododendron Food twice a year in cold-winter climates, and three times a year in mild-winter climates. Some experts recommend feeding rhododendrons and azaleas when growth starts in the spring, during blooming, and then monthly until August. Camellias should be fed before, during, and after blooming. If azaleas or rhododendrons show yellowed leaves caused by an iron or manganese deficiency, give them a foliar feeding by spraying with Scotts Azalea, Evergreen, Rhododendron, Holly Food.

All prefer good drainage and moist soil.

Amend the soil heavily with Scotts Azalea, Camellia & Rhododendron Soil when planting, and never allow the soil to dry out completely. When planting rhododendrons, azaleas, and camellias in containers, use Scotts Azalea, Camellia & Rhododendron Planting Soil.

Thousands of varieties are available.

Camellias have a half-dozen different flower shapes. Some rhododendrons have fragrant flowers or fragrant foliage, and azaleas come in a range of colors from white to pink to yellow, not to mention multicolored varieties. Make your garden a mix of unusual and choice varieties as well as the old standards.

---

a minimum in the spring; and it helps the soil stay cool and moist through the summer. Replace mulches around perennials in the fall in regions with severe winters and in the spring in mild-winter climates. Keep mulches 2 to 3 inches away from the stem to discourage pests and diseases. Look for mulches made of pine-bark nuggets, cypress, or pine bark. Mulches are not only very practical in keeping up with garden weeding, watering, and helping to balance soil temperature, but they look nice, too.

WATERING

The rule of thumb for watering perennials is to water them thoroughly and let the soil dry out between waterings. One sure way to know if the soil is well watered is to take a trowel and dig down to see if the soil is saturated 3 or 4 inches deep. If it is, the water is reaching the root zone. Insufficient watering causes roots to grow upward to find moisture. Such roots can neither feed the plant effectively nor anchor it properly.

The easiest way to water perennials is with a drip-irrigation system set on a timer. Alternatively, a soaker hose is good for watering perennials because, like a drip-irrigation system, it keeps water at the roots and off the foliage where moisture can encourage fungus and disease. Overhead watering to rinse dust off leaves is best done in the morning so the foliage can dry before nightfall.

STAKING

If you are planting perennials that are inclined to flop, you'll save time and trouble (as well as possible root damage) if you put in stakes when planting. Tall, single-stemmed plants, such as delphinium, hollyhock, and gladiolus, need sturdy poles to keep them upright, especially in windy locations. Push the stake into the soil hard enough so it's stable, and tie the stalk to the stake with a plant tie (green plastic tape or horticultural string), forming a figure eight with the tie. Allow enough slack for natural back-and-forth movement.

Bushy perennials that are inclined to get their faces in the mud, such as asters, chrysanthemums, carnations, and peonies, can be grown through slim, plastic-coated metal interlocking stakes that form a cage to keep them standing up. Such stakes are virtually invisible by the time the plants are mature.

Single metal stakes that are coated with green plastic and that have an open loop at the top work well for pulling the occasional errant branch into line. They come in a variety of sizes from 1 to 4 feet tall, and are slender enough that they do minimal root damage when inserted.

WEEDING

The easiest way to keep perennial beds cleared of weeds is to prevent them from coming up in the first place by applying a thick mulch. Pull weeds while they are still small, and preferably when the ground is wet; weeds are much harder to extract when they are large and the soil is hard and dry. To keep your garden-tending well in hand, pull a few weeds every time you're in the garden.

PINCHING

Perennials are pinched to create a shapelier plant, bushier growth, and more flowers. Pinching ordinarily means to nip out the new leaves and buds at the end of each branch. Some perennials, such as chrysanthemums, need to be pinched back several times during the growing season to make full, heavily flowering plants.

FEEDING

A midsummer feeding benefits most herbaceous perennials. Scotts® granular All-Purpose Plant Food or Flower Food can help ensure plants have all the nutrients they need to grow and bloom well. Scotts ready-to-use liquid All-Purpose Plant Food is useful for any individual plants that appear to be lagging. It also can be sprayed on plants as a foliar feeding. Liquid solutions typically are faster acting than dry fertilizers.

A midsummer feeding benefits most perennials, such as larkspur and daisies. Many gardeners prefer to make two applications to keep their flowers in full bloom.

DIVIDING

Gardeners divide perennials for any of three reasons: size control, rejuvenation, and propagation. Left to their own devices, most perennials grow larger every year. They may eventually grow larger than the space allotted for them. Or they may begin to die out at the center and no longer look attractive. Perhaps you'd just like to make several clumps out of a single large clump.

The rule of thumb is to divide spring- and summer-blooming perennials in late summer or fall and fall-blooming perennials in early spring to give the new plants an entire growing season to reestablish themselves. In regions with severe winters (temperatures below -10°F), divide in early spring so that new divisions are not subjected to harsh weather before they are fully established.

Thoroughly soak the plants a day or two before digging them, which makes the process of digging them out much easier. Trim the plants to 6 inches high to better see what needs to be done. Dig out the clumps, and use a sharp knife to separate each of them into several plants. Discard any dead sections. With really stubborn clumps, insert two spading forks into the center back to back, and press the handles toward each other to pry the clump apart.

Sprinkle some Scotts® Transplant Food or Scotts Flower Food into the hole, replant one of the divisions, and soak it thoroughly. Plant the others elsewhere in the garden or pass them along to a friend.

PROTECTING IN WINTER

Winter protection for perennials ranges from bringing tender plants indoors for the winter to laying down a heavy mulch to wrapping plants in layers of insulating material. It all depends on the severity of your winters. In moderately cold climates, it's a good idea to dig tender bulbs, such as gladiolus or dahlias, and store them in a frost-free place. In very cold climates, protect plants by covering them in 3 to 6 inches of mulch until the worst is past.

To make dividing perennials much easier, soak the plants thoroughly a day or two before digging. Trim the plants to about 6 inches to see what needs to be done, dig out the clump (top), and use a sharp knife to separate it into several plants (center). Sprinkle some Scotts Flower Food or Scotts Transplant Food into the hole, replant one of the divisions (bottom), and soak it thoroughly.

PLANTING ROSES

PREPARING THE SOIL

When planting roses, place in full sun, if possible—certainly no less than six hours of sun a day. Roses grow well in most soils, but you can improve both clay and sandy soils by amending them with organic material, such as Scotts® 3-in-1 Organic Mix or Scotts Rose Planting Soil. If you are planting a bed of roses, see the instructions for "Preparing the Soil" for perennials on page 101. If you are planting in containers, simply use Scotts Rose Planting Soil.

CHOOSING GOOD ROSES

There are two steps to choosing good roses. The first is to determine what types of roses you like, whether antique roses, hybrid tea roses, climbing roses, or another kind. Check with local nurseries, American Rose Society chapters, or public gardens to find out which cultivars grow best in your area. Look for the letter AARS (All-American Rose Selection) on rose labels, or find a list of American Rose Society ratings. The roses with the highest ratings are likely to be the easiest and most gratifying to grow.

The second step in choosing a good rose is to examine the plant itself. Most roses are sold bare-root (without soil around the roots), whether through mail-order catalogs or garden centers. Look for at least three canes (branches) as thick as your thumb with no signs of stress (brown sections) or damage (broken or scraped canes). Canes should be spaced well apart and should not cross over each other. Potted roses should be well shaped and bushy, with no signs of damage or disease.

PLANTING ROSES

The classic rule for planting roses is to dig a $10 hole for a $5 plant. Inflation may have changed the numbers, but the point remains: Dig generously sized holes, about 24 inches wide and 24 inches deep. While you're digging the hole, soak bare-root

Before planting, soak roots of bare-root roses in water overnight (top). Dig a hole 24 inches deep and wide, and mound up soil in the bottom. Line up bud union on the rose with ground level (center). Mound soil around canes and water to keep moist (bottom).

roses in a bucket of water. Trim off any broken roots and remove any damaged or crossing canes. Ideally, the plant should be somewhat vase shaped.

Fill the hole with water and let it drain. For bare-root roses, form a cone of loose soil in the center of the hole, with the point of the cone at soil level. Center the rose over the cone of soil, and fill in with a mixture of loose soil and Scotts Rose Planting Soil. Tamp the soil in between the roots good and hard. Toss in some Scotts Transplant Food according to the instructions on the label. Add enough soil to fill the hole completely. Water thoroughly, and tamp down again (the traditional method is to walk around the rose to firm the soil with your feet). Water one last time.

To plant potted roses, see the instructions for "Transplanting Perennials" on page 102.

MAINTAINING ROSES

MULCHING

Mulch rose beds with bark chips to give them a neat, finished look and to keep weeds to a minimum. If roses are part of a permanent perennial border, the same mulch used for other perennials will do for the roses.

WATERING

Roses will take all the water you can give them, but they won't tolerate wet feet. Translated into English, that means that roses must have fast-draining soil. Soak roses well and allow the soil to dry to moderately moist between waterings. A drip-mist system on a timer is best for watering a rose bed, but a soaker hose also works well. If you're watering by hand, water early in the morning, especially if you're rinsing off the leaves. It's important that the foliage dries before evening to help prevent diseases, such as blackspot, rust, and mildew.

FEEDING

Roses do much better when fertilized heavily, but how often you feed them depends on the kind of soil the roses are planted in. Sandy soils need more fertilizing, and clay soils need less. See the fertilizer chart on page 97 for recommended rose foods and follow the directions on the label to encourage fuller plants and heavier blooming.

In general, feed roses early in the spring just as the bush begins to leaf out, in late spring when the plant is budding, and in midsummer to get the plants through the fall and winter.

Above: After planting roses, prune them back by one-third, and remove any dead or broken wood. This fosters the growth of new, strong canes.

Left: Apply an organic mulch, such as fine bark chips, around and over newly planted canes. When new growth appears, gently spray water on the canes to uncover them.

Left: Disbudding small side buds will give you one large flower per stem on hybrid tea roses. Remove the small buds as they appear. For more even-blooming floribunda roses, remove the central buds as they form.

Below: When you cut fresh flowers or remove spent blooms, cut at a 45-degree angle above a strong five-leaflet leaf. This is where new growth will begin. Be sure to leave at least two sets of leaves on each cane to maintain plant vigor. On new plants, leave as much of the cane as possible.

STAKING

Most roses don't require staking. The one exception is tree roses. They usually come from the nursery already staked and can be planted with the stake as one would transplant any other container plant.

PRUNING

Prune most roses in the spring when the buds begin to swell. Roses that bloom once a year should be pruned right after blooming. Remove all weak, dead, diseased, or damaged branches; cut off dead canes at the base. Trim out any crossing canes or errant branches that are growing into paths or lawn areas. Use a sharp pair of pruning shears and make all pruning cuts just above a bud on the outside of the cane. Angle the pruning cuts at about 45 degrees. Cut healthy canes back to one-third of their length, and cut all canes to the same height. Remove all growth from the trunks of tree roses to maintain their treelike appearance.

CONTROLLING PESTS AND DISEASES

Roses are susceptible to a wide variety of pests and diseases. East of the Rockies, the worst pest is the Japanese beetle. It can be controlled with Scotts® Sevin® Insect Killer. Aphids can be blasted off roses with a strong spray from the hose. The only effective controls for nibbling deer are wire cages around the roses or a high fence around the garden.

Blackspot, rust, and mildew are common rose diseases, but there are many others. Check with your local nursery or garden center for effective controls for whatever ails your roses.

Whenever using an insecticide or fungicide, read the label carefully and follow the instructions explicitly. Use these products with caution and store them out of the reach of children.

PROTECTING IN WINTER

Where winter temperatures drop below 0°F, roses need winter protection. Any number of methods work. Wrap roses in several layers of burlap and tie securely with wire or twine. Make a chicken-wire cage to slip over the plant and fill it with loose mulch, such as shredded leaves. Protect climbing roses by bundling straw or layers of newspapers around the canes with twine, followed by a burlap cover secured with twine. In an unexpected cold snap, old blankets or plastic tarps tossed over the roses probably will get them through the night until you can take more permanent measures.

If temperatures drop below 0°F, remove climber canes from supports; cover with leaves (top left). Small pieces of bark work well around roses as a winter-protecting mulch (top right). In very cold climates, use a cardboard, plastic, or metal cylinder to protect roses. Fill it with mulch, leaves, or newspaper (below).

Near right: Tree roses are especially vulnerable to cold winds and weather. They may either be brought indoors or wrapped. Far right: Wrap burlap around four stakes placed around the tree rose and fill loosely with light mulch or leaves.

PLANTING BULBS

PREPARING THE SOIL

Good drainage is the most important soil requirement for bulbs. A sandy, rich soil is ideal. To prevent bulbs from rotting in heavy clay soils, work in Scotts® Bulb Planting Soil Plus Bone Meal. The same mixture will help sandy soils retain moisture and nutrients.

Prepare the soil for a bed of bulbs as directed in "Preparing the Soil" for annuals on page 98. If you're planting bulbs in clumps throughout the garden, add small amounts of the necessary amendments to each planting hole.

CHOOSING GOOD BULBS

In the garden, the term "bulbs" includes the true bulb (daffodil), corm (crocus), tuber (tuberous begonia), tuberous root (dahlia), and rhizome (bearded iris). Select bulbs exactly as you would a good onion at the supermarket: They should be firm, with no sign of damage or disease. Pick the largest bulbs you can find—they'll produce the most flowers. Daffodils often come with two or three bulbs attached together (each bulb is called a "nose"). Select two-nose and three-nose bulbs for the most daffodils.

In cold climates, plant bulbs as soon as they arrive, if they were ordered from a catalog, or as soon as possible after purchase, if they were bought at a nursery or garden center. In mild climates, plant bulbs in November or December, after the soil has cooled down. Hardy bulbs planted in warm-winter climates need to be prechilled before planting: Pop them into the refrigerator (not the freezer) for 8 to 10 weeks for most bulbs and 12 weeks for tulips.

SETTING IN PLACE

The general rule is to dig a hole three times deeper than the diameter of the bulb at its widest point. If the bulb is 2 inches wide, plant it 6 inches deep. Plant most bulbs point up. Tubers and rhizomes don't have points, so lay them flat and plant them fairly shallowly; bearded iris should be barely below the surface. Plant bulbs in full sun or beneath deciduous trees so the spring warmth will start their growth.

For a natural-looking bed, arrange your bulbs in an informal design (top left). Although bulbs do contain their first season's food supply, they will bloom better in the future if phosphorus-rich bone meal is added to the planting holes (bottom left). If squirrels, chipmunks, or other small animals are digging up your bulbs, sink bulbs into a wire basket or spread chicken wire on top of the planting (above).

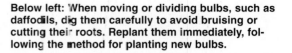
Bulbs look best when massed (many bulbs of one kind in a single bed, such as a bed of red tulips) or in informal drifts, such as when daffodils are naturalized in grassy areas under trees. When planting a row of bulbs, dig a trench, place the bulbs in it, and backfill with loose soil. Line the bottom of the trench with Scotts Bulb Planting Soil Plus Bone Meal. If you are planting bulbs in containers, use Scotts Bulb Planting Soil Plus Bone Meal as the planter mix.

MAINTAINING BULBS

MULCHING

Compost and shredded leaves make good mulches over bulb beds; they help conserve moisture in the soil, and in hot, dry regions, keep soil cool. In cold-winter regions, mulch helps prevent heaving from the freezing and thawing of the earth, which can throw bulbs out of the ground and ruin their growth

Below left: When moving or dividing bulbs, such as daffodils, dig them carefully to avoid bruising or cutting their roots. Replant them immediately, following the method for planting new bulbs.

Below top: In the late fall, mulch over your bulb beds with leaves or other organic mulch. Label the bed in case you forget what you planted where.

Below bottom: When planting a mass of bulbs (which is the way most bulbs look best), dig one large planting hole rather than individual ones. Make the hole 9 to 12 inches deep, and then refill it with loose soil and Scotts Bulb Food or bone meal until the depth is correct for the kind of bulbs you are planting.

and bloom for the season. Mulches also keep weeds to a minimum. Any ground-bark product makes a decorative mulch, which can be dug into the soil to improve it.

WATERING

Water bulbs well when they are planted. Allow the soil to dry, and then water thoroughly. Remember that the water must reach the root zone at the bottom of the planting hole, often 6 inches down. Bulbs in containers must be watered regularly, allowing the pot to dry out between waterings. Most bulbs will survive on natural rainfall or normal garden watering once they are established.

STAKING

Tall, sturdy wooden stakes are necessary for certain summer lilies and large dahlias. These plants can grow to 6 feet and higher. Put the stakes in at the time the bulbs are planted, then tie up the stalks when they grow tall enough to need support. See the instructions for staking plants on page 103.

Smaller bulbs, such as daffodils, can be staked with wire stakes that have an open loop at the top for the stem. These wire stakes are very slender, so they can be inserted when they're needed. They come in a range of heights from 1 to 4 feet. These same stakes also are useful for bulbs that have been planted in containers, because they take up so little room. Be careful not to pierce the bulbs when inserting wire stakes.

FEEDING

Fertilizer with bone meal should be applied to bulb beds or tucked into the bottom of planting holes when bulbs are first planted. Use Scotts® All-Natural Bone Meal or Scotts Bulb Food. After the first year, fertilize bulbs at the beginning of the

Top: If you can't stand the unruly looks of ripening bulb foliage, braid it.

Far left: When bulbs have finished their spring bloom, cut off their seed heads to direct energy to the bulbs for bigger, stronger, better blooms next year.

Near left: Small buds that form at the side of a daffodil bulb can be gently pulled off and replanted. In time, they will be as strong and bright as their parent plant.

Right: Annuals planted around bulbs hide the dying foliage and keep weeds down.

growing season when the first green tips appear. Use Scotts Bulb Food.

The foliage on bulbs must be left on the plant until it yellows. This allows the bulb to store up energy from the sun, water, and soil so that it will set buds and bloom the following year. If messy foliage is bothersome, you may braid it to make it look tidy, but it may interfere with the process of ripening. It's a good idea to feed bulbs once the leaves start to yellow. Scotts Bulb Food is great for this; just scratch it into the soil and water well.

Bulbs grown in containers can be planted in the garden once they are past bloom. Fertilize them and let the foliage ripen naturally. They may not bloom the first year, but usually will come back after that.

WEEDING

Spread mulch in bulb beds to keep weeds down. If you cannot bear the appearance of the dying foliage, overplant the bulbs with annuals to hide it. This also will help crowd out weeds. Classic combinations are blue forget-me-nots planted with red tulips or yellow daffodils planted with white sweet alyssum. Pull weeds when they're small. Pulling large weeds may tumble bulbs out of the soil. If you use a weeding fork, be careful not to pierce nearby bulbs.

DIVIDING

Many bulbs—such as daffodils, grape hyacinth, and English bluebells—will multiply, increasing the number of flowers every year. When the blooms start to get fewer and smaller, it's time to dig the bulbs up and divide them. In most cases, all that needs to be done is to recondition the soil with compost and bulb food, and replant the bulbs farther apart. When dividing bearded irises in late summer, cut the rhizomes apart, and let dry for 24 hours to form a sort of thin scab before replanting. Use Scotts Bulb Planting Soil Plus Bone Meal and Scotts Bulb Food.

Any bulbs that won't fit without crowding can be planted elsewhere or given away. Ordinarily, bulbs need to be divided only every few years.

PROTECTING IN WINTER

Many bulbs, such as crocuses, tulips, daffodils, summer lilies, hyacinths, snowflakes, and glory-of-the-snow, are hardy. All the winter protection they need is a layer of mulch. Use shredded leaves, compost, or chipped wood bark.

STORING TENDER BULBS

Tender bulbs, such as dahlias, freesias, some kinds of tulips, and amaryllis, need to be dug and stored over the winter in cold climates. Dig the bulbs and let them dry for a few days after digging. Pack them in dry sawdust, perlite, or vermiculite in a perforated plastic bag, then store them someplace where temperatures range between 40° and 50°F, such as a heated garage, basement, or sunroom. Label the bags at the time that you pack them, so in the spring you will know whether they are the red tulips or the pink ones, the yellow daffodils or the white jonquils. Plant them out in the spring after the ground has thawed.

In mild climates, the opposite may be required. Summer lilies, for example, may need to be dug every two or three years, placed in paper bags, and chilled in the refrigerator for the winter. Just replant the lilies in early spring, and they'll continue to bloom well.

PLANTING AND MAINTAINING WILDFLOWERS

SEEDING

Wildflower seeds often are sold in mixes of many different wildflowers, both annuals and perennials. Prepare the soil as suggested for perennials on page 101. Wildflower seeds usually are broadcast by hand. The seed packet or can will have the proper instructions on the label. Observe any recommendations regarding sun or shade and moist or dry soil. And be sure the wildflower mix you choose is suitable for your climate.

Another option is Scotts® PatchMaster® Wildflower Garden Seeding Mix, which contains seed, mulch, and fertilizer in one product. Simply spread it over well-prepared soil, and water.

MULCHING

Most wildflowers don't require mulching, because they already are well adapted to the climate; it's how they acquired their name and characteristics, namely sowing themselves and thriving with no human care. The single exception might be woodland wildflowers, for which a light mulch of shredded leaves probably is sufficient.

WATERING

Wildflowers are a good choice in areas where water conservation is an important issue. Because they are adapted, they don't require much water beyond natural rainfall; they certainly don't need more water than normal garden watering provides, which is watering the soil well and allowing it to dry out between waterings. Keep in mind when you do water your wildflowers that deep watering is best. Shallow, frequent waterings cause shallow root growth—and therefore weak plants. Deep watering create deep, strong roots and plants.

DEADHEADING

Wildflowers need to be kept tidy, just as other garden ornamentals do. Dead flowers must be trimmed off before they go to seed to keep the plants blooming longer. If they are allowed to go to seed, it's likely that the most vigorous plants eventually will take over the bed. Good grooming, such as removing dead leaves, withered stems, and unwanted seed heads, will keep wildflowers looking attractive and in top condition.

FEEDING

Fertilize wildflowers lightly (use half of the recommended amount) before blooming and again in late summer after most of the wildflowers have finished blooming. Use a general fertilizer, such as Scotts All-Purpose Plant Food.

WEEDING

Keep wildflower plantings well weeded. Wildflower meadow gardens or prairie gardens are beautiful as long as they are carefully tended. Mixing wildflowers with ornamental grasses helps crowd weeds out, and creates the lovely light patterns and movement of meadows. The easiest way to keep weeds from getting out of hand is to weed wildflowers on a regular basis. Little weeds are easier to remove than big ones, and moist soil is easier to weed than dry. Do your weeding a few hours after a soaking summer rain or after the garden has been watered.

Top: To plant a wildflower garden, spade or till the site to a depth of 8 or 9 inches, removing weeds by hand as you work. Mix in a good compost and peat moss to loosen and improve the soil.

Center: Provide a water source. An in-ground sprinkler system made of PVC pipe is ideal, but a portable garden sprinkler works very well.

Bottom: Mix wildflower seeds with sand for even distribution or use Scotts PatchMaster Wildflower; scatter sparsely by hand. Very lightly cover the seeds with fine soil. For good germination, keep the soil moist with a light spray (to avoid washing the seeds out of the soil).

Answers to Commonly Asked Questions

FLOWER GARDENING, EVEN FOR THE MOST EXPERIENCED, CAN PRESENT A VARIETY OF questions. You may be lucky enough to have a neighbor who can answer your questions across the garden gate. If you don't, here's the next-best thing. Listed below are some of the most commonly asked questions—and their answers—about establishing and maintaining a beautifully blooming flower garden.

Q: Which of the spring-flowering bulbs are best for permanent plantings?

A: Daffodils or narcissus are the most reliable bulbs. They are extremely hardy, and naturalize, or multiply, easily. If you plant 50 daffodil bulbs one year, within a few years, you may have double or more. If you don't have a rodent problem (they love to dig up tender bulbs and eat them), fragrant hyacinth, lily, allium, and little bulbs, such as snowdrop, crocus, grape hyacinth, and scilla, will grow and multiply almost indefinitely. Tulips will bloom about three years or so before they need to be dug up, split, and replanted. Scotts® Bulb Food worked into the soil at planting time and immediately post-bloom will prolong and improve the blossoming of your tulips.

Q: When is the best time to dig up and divide naturalizing bulbs, such as irises and daffodils, and spring-blooming flowers, such as peonies?

A: Early fall is the best time to divide your spring-blooming flowers. You want to do it late enough in the season so that the foliage has had time to soak up nutrients to save up for next year's bloom, but early enough so that the transplants can develop a strong and healthy root system before cold weather hits. In the cold-winter zone, this usually is in September—about the same time you would plant new bulbs. For peony transplants, try working Scotts Transplant Food into the soil; for bulbs, use Scotts Bulb Food.

Q: What kinds of annuals are the easiest to care for?

A: Most annuals are low-maintenance, but some are easier than others. Try marigold, gaillardia, verbena, cleome, cosmos, petunia, salvia, zinnia, annual phlox, sweet alyssum, and impatiens. Most of these plants will bloom quite late into the season with just watering, weeding, deadheading (removing spent flower heads to encourage more bloom), and feedings with Scotts® Flower Food to keep them thriving.

Q: Which annuals are best to plant when I want height at the back of my beds?

A: The best annuals for background planting are tall ones, such as amaranthus, celosia, cleome, cosmos, larkspur, tall varieties of marigold, salvia, tall varieties of snapdragon, and zinnia. Many of these varieties also make good cut flowers, with their sturdy stems that let them stand so tall in the back of your garden.

Q: What kind of soil mixture do I need for successfully starting flower seeds indoors?

A: You need a mix of one part soil, one part peat moss, and one part sand, vermiculite or sphagnum moss, or use Scotts Seed Starter Potting Soil, which is a rich mixture of these organic materials. The best way to ensure that the mix is sterile and has all of the nutrients tender seedlings require is to use Scotts Seed Starter Potting Soil. It is specifically blended to germinate and grow seeds, and contains a wetting agent that promotes even wetting of soil. It's also ideal for establishing root and stem cuttings.

Q: What is deadheading?

A: Deadheading is the process of pinching off the spent flower blooms on annuals, biennials, and perennials. If you deadhead a flower as soon as it is brown and drooping, you will get longer and healthier blooms. Otherwise, the plant will begin to set seed, which takes energy the plant could be using to produce more colorful blooms to enliven your garden.

Q: What are biennials?

A: Biennials are plants, such as foxglove and hollyhock, that begin their life cycle one season and complete it the next. Biennials generally germinate and establish healthy roots and foliage one year and then bloom the following year, when they produce and scatter seed to start the whole cycle all over again. So, although the same plant won't return year after year, as with perennials, it is possible to have perennially blooming biennials by allowing them to self-seed.

Q: **What kinds of perennials grow in the shade?**

A: Actually, there are quite a few beautiful choices of perennials to grow in the shade. Some of the best include monkshood, ajuga, anemone, astilbe, bleeding-heart, bugbane, Carpathian bluebell, daylily, fern, lily-of-the-valley, lobelia, phlox, hosta, plumbago, primrose, vinca, and violet.

Q: **What is a good plan for year-round care of my perennial border?**

A: In the spring, as soon as the danger of frost is over, remove the mulch or winter protection. If you use a fine organic material, much of it can be worked into the soil, along with a good basic fertilizer, such as Scotts® Flower Food. You can divide perennials and replant, as well as reset any plants that were lifted out of the bed by freezing and thawing. Weed and, if desired, mulch again to suppress weed growth and conserve water. Throughout the season, keep the bed free of weeds and thoroughly watered. In the fall, winterize the garden by cutting down dead foliage and, after the ground is frozen, mulching over for the winter.

Q: **What kind of soil do roses like best?**

A: Roses like a slightly acidic soil that has very good drainage—they don't like wet feet. It's also a good idea, particularly if you have sandy soil, to work an abundance of organic material into the soil and to apply at least three applications of a good fertilizer throughout the growing season—one in the early spring, one in June (about the time of peak bloom), and one in August. Scotts Rose Food is an excellent choice.

Q: **How can I control pests on my roses?**

A: Roses are lovely, but unfortunately, they fall prey to many an insect pest. The best way to control those pests is to apply a good insect killer. Sevin® Insect Killer from Scotts kills nearly 100 different kinds of pests that attack roses.

Q: **How much water should I give my roses?**

A: Although roses don't like to stand in sitting water, they do like plenty of water that drains well. They will grow better and produce more and better blooms if they are thoroughly watered once a week. That means the water should soak down at least 5 or 6 inches to be most effective. Shallow waterings leave your roses open to disease and prevent healthy root growth, as the roots will grow down only as far as you water. Deep waterings mean deep-reaching, strong roots.

Plant Alternatives

B USING THE CHART BELOW, NEARLY EVERY PLAN IN THIS BOOK CAN BE MADE TO FIT EVERY climate region. The second column lists the plants that appear in the plans as shown on pages 6-95. Alternatives for designated regions are listed to the right of that column. Plants appearing on the plan pages, but not below, are suited to all three regions.

PLAN/PAGE	ORIGINAL PLANTS LISTED	ALTERNATIVES	
1. Edgings Pgs. 6-7	*Note: In Region A, columbine should be Aquilegia canadensis.*		
2. Edgings Pgs. 8-9	*Note: No substitutes needed.*		
3. Front Entry Pg. 10	**Plants for Regions A, B, & C** Pinks Campanula Lavender Climbing roses	**Alternatives for Region A** Speedwell *(Veronica spicata)*	**Alternatives for Region C** Vervain *(Verbena rigida)* Ground morning glory Bougainvillea
	Note: In the coldest parts of Region A, substitute speedwell for the lavender. In the warmest parts of Region C, make the above-noted substitutions for best results.		
4. Front Entry Pg. 11	**Plants for Region C** Coral tree *(Erythrina)* Amur privet *(Ligustrum amurense)* Creeping fig *(Ficus pumila)*	**Alternatives for Regions A & B** Red horse chestnut *(Aesculus X carnea)* Japanese privet *(Ligustrum japonicum 'Rotundifolium')* Boston ivy *(Parthenocissus tricuspidata)*	
5. Foundation Pgs. 12-13	**Plants for Regions B & C** Evergreen clematis *(Clematis armandii)* Mexican orange *(Choisya ternata)*	**Alternatives for Region A** Silver lace vine *(Polygonum aubertii)* Hills-of-snow *(Hydrangea arborescens 'Grandiflora')*	
	Note: In Region C, tulip and squill should be replanted annually or replaced with Persian buttercup (Ranunculus asiaticus), also an annual. Spirea is shown in the plan, but glossy abelia works better in most of Regions B and C.		
6. Foundation Pgs. 14-15	**Plants for Regions B & C** Matilija poppies Japanese maple	**Alternatives for Region A** Peony Amur maple	
	Note: In the warmest parts of Region C, the lilies should be handled as annuals or replaced with ginger lily (Hedychium gardnerianum).		
7. Side Yard Pgs. 16-17	**Plants for Region B** Arborvitae Lavender	**Alternatives for Region A** Arborvitae Speedwell *(Veronica spicata)*	**Alternatives for Region C** Yew pine *(Podocarpus macrophyllus)*
	Note: In Region A, the euonymus should be Euonymus alata.		

PLAN/PAGE	ORIGINAL PLANTS LISTED	ALTERNATIVES	
8. Side Yard Pgs. 18-19	**Plants for Region B** Heartleaf crambe Porcelain ampelopsis *(Ampelopsis brevipedvaculata)* Cranesbill geranium	**Alternatives for Region A** Baby's breath *(Gypsophilia paniculata)*	**Alternatives for Region C** Star jasmine *(Trachelospermum jasminoides)* Stokes' aster *(Stokesia laevis)*
	Note: Foxglove and Canterbury bells are risky in the coldest parts of Region A. Dane's-blood bellflower (Campanula glomerata) makes a good substitute. Artemisia stellerana *is recommended for the coldest parts of Region A.*		
9. Quick Results Pgs. 20-21	**Plants for Regions B & C** Boxwood *(Buxus)*	**Alternatives for Region A** *Euonymus alata 'Compacta'*	
10. Low Maintenance Pgs. 22-23	**Plants for Regions A, B, & C** Deciduous magnolia or pink trumpet tree *(Tabebuia impetiginosa)*	**Alternatives for Region A** Crab apple	
	Note: Although a deciduous magnolia is shown for all three regions, a crab apple would be better suited to the coldest parts of Region A. In Region C, the daylilies should be the evergreen type.		
11. Spring Color Pgs. 24-25	**Plants for Regions A & B** Euonymus Dusty miller Crab apple	**Alternatives for Region A** Shrubby cinquefoil *(Potentilla)* Wormwood *(Artemisia stellerana)*	**Alternatives for Region C** Flowering plum *(Prunus sp.)*
	Note: With the above-named plant replacements, this plan is even better suited to the coldest parts of Region A. In Region C, tulips and hyacinths should be replanted annually or replaced with Persian buttercup (Ranunculus asiaticus).		
12. Summer and Fall Color Pgs. 26-27	**Plants for Regions A, B, & C** Erodium	**Alternatives for Region A** Dragon's blood sedum *(Sedum spurium)*	
	Note: In Region A, almost all plants will be handled as annuals. The dragon's blood sedum is better suited to the cold than erodium.		
13. Fall Color Pgs. 28-29	**Plants for Region A** Marguerite daisy	**Alternatives for Regions B & C** Golden marguerite *(Anthemis tinctoria)*	
	Note: The marguerite daisies should be handled as annuals in Region A, or replaced by golden marguerite, a perennial.		
14. 3-Season Color Pgs. 30-31	*Note: The campanula is marginally successful in the warmest parts of Region C, but can be handled as an annual during the cool months and replaced with a white-flowered form of vinca (Catharanthus roseus) during the hot months.*		
15. Perennial Border Pg. 32	**Plants for Regions A & B** Phlox Primrose Goldenrod	**Alternatives for Region A** Golden marguerite *(Anthemis tinctoria)*	**Alternatives for Region C** Red valerian *(Centranthus ruber)* Primrose Butterfly weed *(Asclepias tuberosa)*
	Note: If primrose is used in Region A, it should be Japanese star primrose, or replaced with golden marguerite.		
16. Perennial Border Pg. 33	**Plants for Regions A & B** Phlox *(Phlox paniculata)* Bugbane *(Cimicifuga simplex)* Rocket ligularia *(Ligularia X przewalskii 'The Rocket')* Campanula	**Alternatives for Region C** Shasta daisy *(Chrysanthemum X superbum)* Canna *(Canna X generalis)* Red hot poker *(Kniphofia uvaria)* Pitcher's sage *(Salvia azurea grandiflora)*	
	Note: In the coldest parts of Region A, replace perennial sunflower with yarrow.		
17. Annual Border Pgs. 34-35	**Plants for Region C** New Zealand tea tree *(Leptospermum scoparium)*	**Alternatives for Regions A & B** Tartarian honeysuckle *(Lonicera tartarica)*	
	Note: If ice plant is not locally available, calendula makes a fine substitute.		

PLAN/PAGE	ORIGINAL PLANTS LISTED	ALTERNATIVES	
18. Mixed Border Pgs. 36-37	**Plants for Regions A & B** *Phlox paniculata* (white) *Phlox paniculata* (pink) Golden marguerite *(Anthemis tinctoria)*	**Alternatives for Region C** Shasta daisy Red valerian *(Centranthus ruber)* Marguerite daisy	
	Note: In Region A, the artemisia should be A. stellerana to be perennial, otherwise any artemisia will do.		
19. Cottage Garden Pgs. 38-39	**Plants for Regions A & B** Peony Potentilla Arborvitae	**Alternatives for Region C** Daylily (evergreen forms) Marguerite *(Chrysanthemum frutescens)* Shrubby yew pine *(Podocarpus macrophyllus maki)*	
	Note: In Region C, use Dicentra 'Luxuriant' as the bleeding heart.		
20. Bird and Butterfly Garden Pgs. 40-41	*Note: In Region C, use evergreen daylilies.*		
21. Formal Garden Pgs. 42-43	**Plants for Region B & C** Boxwood *(Buxus)*	**Alternatives for Region A** Shrubby cinquefoil *(Potentilla)* or germander *(Teucrium chamaedrys)*	
	Note: Lavender, lavender cotton, and feverfew may be handled as annuals in colder climates. Signet marigold and lovage are annuals in all climates.		
22. Informal Garden Pgs. 44-45	*Note: Except in the warmest parts of Region C—where they will grow as perennials—handle these as annuals: fuchsia, cineraria, daisies (Chrysanthemum paludosum), and California poppy. Palm is suited for Region C only.*		
23. Naturalized Garden Pgs. 46-47	*Note: There is no substitute for the palm in Regions A & B. In Region C the daylilies should be the evergreen type. In the coldest parts of Region C, replace the lantana with Bumald spirea (Spiraea X bumalda).*		
24. Island Beds Pgs. 48-49	**Plants for Region C** Carnation Blue marguerite *(Felicia amelloides)* Lavender	**Alternatives for Region A** Gas plant *(Dictamnus albus 'Rubus' and 'Purpureus')* Bigroot cranesbill *(Geranium macrorrhizum)* Speedwell *(Veronica spicata)*	**Alternatives for Region B** Bigroot cranesbill
25. Small Space Pgs. 50-51	**Plants for Region C** Cape plumbago *(Plumbago auriculata)* *Note: Use larkspur as an annual.*	**Alternatives for Regions A & B** *Phlox paniculata* (lavender color)	
26. Small Space Pgs. 52-53	**Plants for Regions A, B, & C** Silver lace vine *(Polygonum aubertii)* *Delphinium belladonna*	**Alternatives for Region C** Pink jasmine *(Jasminum polyanthum)* Pitcher's sage *(Salvia azurea grandiflora)*	
	Note: This plan is suited to all three climate regions, but the above substitutes make it better suited to Region C. Handle these as annuals: geranium, petunia, dusty miller, zinnia, and scaevola. Scaevola and geraniums will grow as perennials in dry-summer areas of Region C. If Delphinium belladonna is used in Region C, it will be a short-lived perennial.		
27. Large Space Pgs. 54-55	**Plants for Regions A & B** Delphinium Lupine Poppy	**Alternatives for Region C** Pitcher's sage *(Salvia azurea grandiflora)* Cardinal flower *(Lobelia cardinalis)* Shirley poppy (as an annual)	
	Note: Foxglove is risky in the coldest parts of Region A.		

PLAN/PAGE	ORIGINAL PLANTS LISTED	ALTERNATIVES	
28. High Altitude Pgs. 56-57	**Plants for Regions A & B** Colorado blue spruce Astilbe Summer phlox	**Alternatives for Region C** Blue Atlas cedar *(Cedrus atlantica glauca)* False dragonhead *(Physostegia)* Red valerian *(Centranthus ruber)* or Spiderwort *(Tradescantia X andersoniana)*	
29. Slope Pgs. 58-59	**Plants for Region C** *Grevillea 'Noelli'* Mock orange *(Pittosporum)* Pink marguerite	**Alternatives for Region A** Juniper Shrubby cinquefoil *(Potentilla)* Bigroot cranesbill *(Geranium macrorrhizum)*	**Alternatives for Region B** Juniper Boxwood Bigroot cranesbill *(Geranium macrorrhizum)*
	Note: In Region A, forget-me-not should be Myosotis sylvatica, and columbine should be Aquilegia canadensis.		
30. Poor Soil Pg. 60	**Plants for Regions B & C** Perennial flax *(Linum perenne)*	**Alternatives for Region A** Creeping phlox *(Phlox divaricata)*	
	Note: In the coldest parts of Region A, replace red hot poker with cardinal flower.		
31. Poor Soil Pg. 61	*Note: No plant substitutes necessary, if santolina and lavender are handled as annuals in Region A. In Region A, santolina may be replaced with tansy (Tanacetum vulgare).*		
32. Dry Climate Pgs. 62-63	**Plants for Region C** Ice plant *(Lampranthus spectabilis)* Sea lavender *(Limonium)*	**Alternatives for Regions A & B** Calendula Chinese forget-me-not *(Cynoglossum amabile)*	
	Note: In Regions A and B, replace aloe, agave, and cactus with soapweed and red hot poker.		
33. Front Entry Pgs. 64-65	**Plants for Region C** Star jasmine *(Trachelospermum jasminoides)* Lily-of-the-Nile *(Agapanthus)*	**Alternatives for Regions A & B** Snowberry *(Symphoricarpos albus)* *Allium caeruleum* or Stars-of-Persia *(Allium christophii)*	
34. Front Entry Pgs. 66-67	**Plants for Regions A & B** Maple	**Alternatives for Region C** Oak	
	Note: In Regions A and B, ferns must be a winter-hardy species, such as lady fern, ostrich fern, or cinnamon fern.		
35. Side Yard Pgs. 68-69	**Plants for Regions B & C** Evergreen magnolia Azalea	**Alternatives for Region A** Summersweet clethra PJM rhododendron hybrid	
	Note: In the warmest parts of Region C, the iris should be a Louisiana hybrid type.		
36. Side Yard Pgs. 70-71	**Plants for Regions B & C** Azalea Miscanthus	**Alternatives for Region A** PJM rhododendron Tufted hairgrass	
37. Foundation Pg. 72	**Plants for Region B** Holly Lily Feverfew Solomon's seal	**Alternatives for Region A** Mountain ash *(Sorbus aucuparia)*	**Alternatives for Region C** Ginger lily *(Hedychium gardneranum)* Lilyturf (white flower form) Spiderwort *(Tradescantia X andersoniana)*
	Note: The above-listed substitutes make the plan better suited to Regions A and C. In coldest parts of Region A, replace the Solomon's seal with bleeding heart (Dicentra spectabilis).		
38. Foundation Pg. 73	*Note: Impatiens, begonias, and coleus should be handled as annuals.*		

PLAN/PAGE	ORIGINAL PLANTS LISTED	ALTERNATIVES	
39. Edgings Pg. 74	**Plants for Regions B & C** Dogwood Azalea Cotoneaster Japanese maple	**Alternatives for Region A** Serviceberry (Amelanchier laevis) Sheep laurel or PJM rhododendron hybrid Bearberry (Arctostaphylos uva-ursi) Amur maple (Acer ginnala)	
	Note: Use the verbena and houttuynia as annuals in the coldest parts of Region A. In the warmest parts of Region C, replace the gooseneck loosestrife with poor man's rhododendron (Impatiens oliveri). The miniature rose will require winter protection in Region A. To be fully hardy, the yucca should be soapweed (Yucca glauca).		

40. Edgings
Pg. 75
	Plants for Regions A & B
	Rocket ligularia
	Pearly everlasting (Anaphalis
	   margaritacea)
		Alternatives for Region C
		Flowering maple (Abutilon X hybridum)
		Poor man's rhododendron
		   (Impatiens oliveri)	

41. Quick Results Pgs. 76-77	**Plants for Region C** Lily-of-the-Nile (Agapanthus)	**Alternatives for Regions A & B** Allium caeruleum or Stars-of-Persia (Allium christophii)	
42. Low Maintenance Pgs. 78-79	*Note: Impatiens should be handled as an annual, and the ferns can be overwintered indoors where they aren't cold-hardy. For winter-hardy ferns, use Christmas fern in Regions A and B.*		
43. Low Maintenance Pgs. 80-81	**Plants for Regions B & C** Leadwort (Ceratostigma plumbaginoides)	**Alternatives for Region A** Wild sweet william (Phlox divaricata)	
44. Woodland Garden Pgs. 82-83	**Plants for Region B** Azalea Violet (Violet odorata) Mayapple (Podophyllum peltatum)	**Alternatives for Region A** PJM rhododendron hybrid Creeping phlox (Phlox stolonifera)	**Alternatives for Region C** Cast iron plant (Aspidistra elatior)
45. Cottage Garden Pgs. 84-85	**Plants for Region B** Dogwood (Cornus)	**Alternatives for Region A** Crabapple (Malus) or Serviceberry (Amelanchier laevis)	**Alternatives for Region C** Orchid tree (Bauhinia variegata)
46. Informal Garden Pgs. 86-87	**Plants for Regions A & B** Dwarf red leaf Japanese barberry Campanula Lady's-mantle	**Alternatives for Region C** Dwarf heavenly bamboo (Nandina domestica 'Nana Purpurea') Mist flower (Eupatorium coelestinum) Calceolaria (Calceolaria crenatiflora)	
47. Perennial Border Pgs. 88-89	**Plants for Regions B & C** Variegated euonymus	**Alternatives for Region A** Shrubby St. John's-wort (Hypericum prolificum)	
	Note: Hosta and astilbe will be short-lived in the warmest parts of Region C. Hosta can be replaced with caladium (Caladium bicolor) in those areas.		
48. Dry Climate Pgs. 90-91	**Plants for Regions A & B** Lily	**Alternatives for Region C** Calla lily (Zantedeschia aethiopica)	
49. Slope Pgs. 92-93	**Plants for Regions A & B** Daylily White birch (Betula pendula)	**Alternatives for Region C** Ginger lily (Hedychium gardneranum) River birch (Betula nigra)	
50. Large Space Pgs. 94-95	*Note: In the warmest parts of Region C, the daylilies should be evergreen varieties. In the coldest parts of Region A, the rhododendron should be one of the PJM hybrids.*		

Index

Scotts®
See & Do Solutions™
Flower Gardens

Editor in Chief
Don Johnson

Senior Project Editor
James D. Blume

Design Director
Deetra Polito

**Contributing
Project Editor**
Lisa Kingsley

**Contributing
Project Designer and
Illustrator**
Eric Groves

**Assistant Contributing
Project Designer**
Carol M. Berg

Contributing Writers
Sara Godwin
Linda Joan Smith

**Contributing
Horticulturist**
Tom Eltzroth

**Contributing
Landscape Architect**
Jane Timm

Contributing Indexer
Elinor Lindheimer

Contributing Copy Edito
Dave Kirchner

Editorial Assistant
Joan Worzala

Publication Managers
Mike Peterson
Fred Tietze

**Creative and Marketing
Sevices Director**
Alison Jaret

**Marketing Services
Manager**
Susan Jaeger

Production Manager
Ivan McDonald

GOOD ON ALL SCOTTS PURCHASES

See & Do SOLUTIONS™ **Refund Certificate**

Offer limit $2.
Minimum purchase $5.

HOW TO OBTAIN YOUR REFUND:

SAMPLE

1. Buy any Scotts product including Scotts tools. Minimum purchase $5.
2. Save your dated cash register receipt.
3. Clip proof of purchase from product package (see illustration at left). Photocopies and facsimiles not accepted.

4. Mail this certificate, the original or a copy of your cash register receipt, and required proof of purchase to address at right. All 3 items must be enclosed to qualify. Certificates cannot be photocopied, reduced, or reprinted. This offer cannot be combined with other Scotts rebate offers.

Mail to: Scotts See & Do Solutions Refund
P.O. Box 1074
Young America, MN 55594-1074
Maximum of $20 per name, household, or address

PLEASE TYPE OR PRINT CLEARLY

NAME

ADDRESS

CITY/STATE   ZIP

Offer good only in U.S.A. where not prohibited, taxed, or restricted by law. Cannot be combined with other offers. Please allow 5 to 6 weeks for delivery.

See & Do SOLUTIONS™ **Refund Certificate**

Offer limit $2.
Minimum purchase $5.

HOW TO OBTAIN YOUR REFUND:

SAMPLE

1. Buy any Scotts product including Scotts tools. Minimum purchase $5.
2. Save your dated cash register receipt.
3. Clip proof of purchase from product package (see illustration at left). Photocopies and facsimiles not accepted.

4. Mail this certificate, the original or a copy of your cash register receipt, and required proof of purchase to address at right. All 3 items must be enclosed to qualify. Certificates cannot be photocopied, reduced, or reprinted. This offer cannot be combined with other Scotts rebate offers.

Mail to: Scotts See & Do Solutions Refund
P.O. Box 1074
Young America, MN 55594-1074
Maximum of $20 per name, household, or address

PLEASE TYPE OR PRINT CLEARLY

NAME

ADDRESS

CITY/STATE   ZIP

Offer good only in U.S.A. where not prohibited, taxed, or restricted by law. Cannot be combined with other offers. Please allow 5 to 6 weeks for delivery.

SAVE UP TO $10

See & Do SOLUTIONS™ **Refund Certificate**

Offer limit $2.
Minimum purchase $5.

HOW TO OBTAIN YOUR REFUND:

SAMPLE

1. Buy any Scotts product including Scotts tools. Minimum purchase $5.
2. Save your dated cash register receipt.
3. Clip proof of purchase from product package (see illustration at left). Photocopies and facsimiles not accepted.

4. Mail this certificate, the original or a copy of your cash register receipt, and required proof of purchase to address at right. All 3 items must be enclosed to qualify. Certificates cannot be photocopied, reduced, or reprinted. This offer cannot be combined with other Scotts rebate offers.

Mail to: Scotts See & Do Solutions Refund
P.O. Box 1074
Young America, MN 55594-1074
Maximum of $20 per name, household, or address

PLEASE TYPE OR PRINT CLEARLY

NAME

ADDRESS

CITY/STATE   ZIP

Offer good only in U.S.A. where not prohibited, taxed, or restricted by law. Cannot be combined with other offers. Please allow 5 to 6 weeks for delivery.

See & Do SOLUTIONS™ **Refund Certificate**

Offer limit $2.
Minimum purchase $5.

HOW TO OBTAIN YOUR REFUND:

SAMPLE

1. Buy any Scotts product including Scotts tools. Minimum purchase $5.
2. Save your dated cash register receipt.
3. Clip proof of purchase from product package (see illustration at left). Photocopies and facsimiles not accepted.

4. Mail this certificate, the original or a copy of your cash register receipt, and required proof of purchase to address at right. All 3 items must be enclosed to qualify. Certificates cannot be photocopied, reduced, or reprinted. This offer cannot be combined with other Scotts rebate offers.

Mail to: Scotts See & Do Solutions Refund
P.O. Box 1074
Young America, MN 55594-1074
Maximum of $20 per name, household, or address

PLEASE TYPE OR PRINT CLEARLY

NAME

ADDRESS

CITY/STATE   ZIP

Offer good only in U.S.A. where not prohibited, taxed, or restricted by law. Cannot be combined with other offers. Please allow 5 to 6 weeks for delivery.